THE
TEACHING
PORTFOLIO

THE TEACHING PORTFOLIO

*A Practical Guide to
Improved Performance And
Promotion/Tenure Decisions*

PETER SELDIN
Pace University

Anker Publishing Company, Inc.
Bolton, MA

THE TEACHING PORTFOLIO
A Practical Guide to Improved Performance and
Promotion/Tenure Decisions

ISBN 0-9627042-1-0

Composition by AUC Educational Technology Services
Cover design by Barbanel Design, Inc.
Printing and binding by Goodway Graphics

Anker Publishing Company, Inc.
176 Ballville Road
P.O. Box 249
Bolton, MA 01740-0249

ABOUT THE AUTHOR

Peter Seldin is Professor of Management at Pace University, Pleasantville, New York. He received his B.A. degree (1963) in psychology from Hobart and William Smith Colleges, his M.B.A. degree (1966) in management from Long Island University, and his Ph.D. degree (1974) in education from Fordham University. His postdoctoral work in evaluation and development was completed at the University of London in 1976.

Seldin has designed and conducted seminars for faculty and administrators in colleges and universities throughout the United States and in more than twenty countries around the world. He is a frequent speaker at national and international conferences. He has served on the Editorial Board of *Innovative Higher Education*, on the Core Committee of the Professional and Organizational Development Network, on the Program Advisory Committee for the International Conference on Improving University Teaching, and in the National Leadership Group of the American Council on Education.

His books include How COLLEGES EVALUATE PROFESSORS (1975), TEACHING PROFESSORS TO TEACH (1977), SUCCESSFUL FACULTY EVALUATION PROGRAMS (1980), CHANGING PRACTICES IN FACULTY EVALUATION (1984), EVALUATING AND DEVELOPING ADMINISTRATIVE PERFORMANCE (1988), (with associates) How ADMINISTRATORS CAN IMPROVE TEACHING (1990), and he is editor of COPING WITH FACULTY STRESS (1987). He has contributed numerous articles on the teaching profession, the management of higher education, evaluating and developing performance, and academic culture to such publications as the *New York Times* and *Change* magazine.

CONTENTS

FOREWORD

Evaluating college and university teaching is a longstanding problem which has come increasingly into the limelight. In our research on factors influencing promotion decisions at the University of Michigan, we found that most members of promotions committees believed that teaching and research should be weighted equally; yet in reviewing simulated promotion dossiers, their decisions reflected greater weight given to research than to teaching.

The problem seems to be that members of committees determining promotion have less confidence in the evidence on teaching effectiveness than they have in evidence of research productivity. Despite the substantial body of evidence supporting the validity of student ratings of teaching, the ratings are often discounted. Thus if undergraduate teaching is to be rewarded (as recommended in recent statements by national bodies and presidents of universities and foundations), we need to supply more persuasive documentation of teaching effectiveness.

The teaching portfolio offers a promising solution to this problem. The teaching portfolio provides a record of real teaching activities that can be compared to the ideal teaching role as defined by the institution. The portfolio is also the tangible, concrete evidence needed by those responsible for personnel decisions. Moreover, the exercise of preparing a portfolio is likely to stimulate critical self-analysis on the part of the faculty member.

THE TEACHING PORTFOLIO: A PRACTICAL GUIDE TO IMPROVED PERFORMANCE AND PROMOTION/TENURE DECISIONS is a valuable resource both for individual faculty members and for college and university administrators who desire increased recognition of good teaching.

The next step needed is research on the impact of the teaching portfolio on decision making. Does it result in greater weight being given to teaching? Are decisions based on the portfolio more reliable and valid than those made using other methods of assessment? What elements of the portfolio contribute most to the portfolio's value?

What are the costs, as well as the gains, of portfolio assessment as compared with traditional assessment (or lack of assessment)? These are the questions we now need to address.

Wilbert J. McKeachie
Ann Arbor, Michigan
June, 1991

PREFACE

The quality of teaching has become a crucial concern at colleges and universities today. Swelling pressures from such diverse sources as the Carnegie Foundation for the Advancement of Teaching, the American Association for Higher Education, state legislatures, faculty and students have moved institutions to reconsider the importance of teaching and the role of the instructor in the classroom.

Pivotal to this reconsideration is the issue of the reward system. In truth, it does little good to tout teaching excellence if faculty consistently perceive that only research is considered important. If outstanding teaching is to be encouraged, institutions must provide meaningful rewards to faculty for teaching.

But how can professors document superior classroom performance or an outstanding effort to improve performance? The best way I know to provide such documentation is the teaching portfolio. Why? Because it documents both the complexity and individuality of good teaching. Today, the routine approach to evaluating teaching relies almost exclusively on student ratings. Portfolios go well beyond the routine approach. They include documents and materials from a number of important sources. Also, the routine approach to evaluation originates with and is controlled by administration. The portfolio concept, on the other hand, empowers faculty members to take charge of their own evaluations.

The teaching portfolio approach is increasingly recognized and respected. Among the many presidents of academic institutions and associations supporting the portfolio are outgoing Harvard University president Derek C. Bok; Ernest L. Boyer, President of the Carnegie Foundation for the Advancement of Teaching (see SCHOLARSHIP REVISITED, 1990); and Lynne Cheney, Chairman of the National Endowment for the Humanities (see TYRANNICAL MACHINES, 1990).

THE TEACHING PORTFOLIO is a hands-on look at the why, what, and how of preparing and successfully using the portfolio. It offers faculty and administrators ready-to-use and research-based information.

Earlier books on improving teaching effectiveness were mainly collections of instructional techniques, often focused on a specific discipline. This book is different. It focuses squarely on teaching portfolios, which may prove to be the most innovative and promising teaching improvement technique in years. It identifies key issues, red-flag warnings and benchmarks for success. It carefully differentiates between portfolios for personnel decisions and portfolios for teaching improvement. It describes how ten different institutions use portfolios and includes the name of a resource person at each institution. It lists thirty possible portfolio items from which faculty can choose the ones personally most relevant. And it includes eight actual teaching portfolios from across disciplines.

The book does more than provide readers with a distillation of the research literature. It also provides a distillation of the author's personal experience over two decades as an academic dean, department chair, professor of management, and consultant to more than one hundred fifty institutions of higher education in all parts of the United States.

The TEACHING PORTFOLIO is written for presidents, provosts, academic vice presidents, deans, department chairs and faculty members—the essential partners in developing successful teaching evaluation and development programs. The straightforward language, practical suggestions and recommendations should prove valuable whether administrators and faculty are in public or private institutions. The book should also be helpful to graduate students, especially those planning careers as teachers.

Acknowledgements

This book, like nearly all others, builds on the work of many educators. I thank, first, the Canadian Association of University Teachers (CAUT) for its seminal work on teaching dossiers. The collaborative efforts of Bruce Shore (McGill), Stephen Foster (British Columbia), Christopher Knapper (Waterloo), Gilles Nadeau (Moncton), Neill Neill (Guelph) and Victor Sim (CAUT) were instrumental in shaping my thinking.

I also acknowledge a special thanks to Russell Edgerton, president of the American Association for Higher Education. Two years ago, he asked me to write a report on teaching portfolios. I was flat on my back suffering from a herniated disk at the time, and I hesitated. But Russ's persuasive words won out. Since then, he has been a steady source of advice and encouragement.

The contributions of other colleagues should also be noted. Linda Annis, Ball State University; Les Cochran, Southeast Missouri State University; Pat Hutchings, American Association for Higher Education; Mardee Jenrette, Miami–Dade Community College; Robert Menges, Northwestern University; Barbara Millis, University of Maryland; Mary Ann Shea, University of Colorado at Boulder; Marilla Svinicki, University of Texas at Austin, James Wilkinson, Harvard University; Alan Wright, Dalhousie University (Canada); and Kenneth Zahorski, St. Norbert College; strongly believed in the importance of this project. They have been more helpful than they may realize.

Peter Seldin
Croton-on-Hudson, NY
June, 1991

1

THE TEACHING PORTFOLIO

INTRODUCTION

Today, the nation's colleges and universities are attempting to respond to new understandings about what elements define effective teaching. At the same time, they are beset by public pressures to improve their systems of teaching accountability. This introduction briefly describes both challenges and suggests that both can be met, at least in part, through the use of the teaching portfolio.

No one doubts that we are still short many answers to the teaching-learning process. But we do have some of the answers. More than 10,000 studies have been published on one phase or another of teaching effectiveness, and from them we have gleaned some reasonably consistent findings about the general characteristics of good teaching. Briefly, these findings indicate that effective teachers are masters of their subject, can organize and emphasize, can clarify ideas and point out relationships, can motivate students, and are reasonable, open, concerned and imaginative human beings.

There are now fresh understandings about what goes into effective teaching. Shulman (1989a) says that effective teachers recognize the impact of prior knowledge on subsequent learning. They, therefore, connect new information with what students already know through a set of metaphors, analogies, examples, stories and demonstrations. They bridge new and already learned subject matter. Shulman's research leads him to conclude that there is a kind of knowledge uniquely possessed by effective teachers of particular disciplines. Thus, he says, pedagogical content-knowledge transcends

1

mere knowledge of subject matter as well as generic understanding of teaching alone. Edgerton (1989, p. 15) concurs and is persuaded that there is only so much that is important to know about teaching in general. "Teaching is highly context specific," he says, "and its true richness can be fully appreciated only by looking at how we teach a particular subject to a particular set of students."

There is a powerful implication here. Until now, colleges and universities have attempted to strengthen teaching performance through centers for faculty and instructional development that focused on generic methods of instruction. But the new insights into teaching suggest that teaching improvement efforts should be centered in the departments where professors teach.

To further complicate things, at the same time that colleges and universities are busy responding to new understandings about effective teaching, they are confronted by strident demands from community and governmental groups to hold professors accountable for their teaching performance. State legislatures, which fund public colleges and universities, are now taking keen interest in knowing how faculty members allocate their time. Boards of trustees of private institutions are viewing the professional activities of faculty members with closer scrutiny.

Some institutions are being directed to report on the percentage of professional time and salary devoted to teaching. Others are adopting a budgetary process in which each department chair has to justify the salary of each professor. Still others are freezing the granting of tenure and promotion to senior rank. In short, the demand for faculty accountability has become a groundswell sweeping across the nation. It has enlisted taxpayers, institutional trustees, financial donors, parents and students to press colleges and universities to examine the performance of each professor.

At first, the pressure was on to improve systems of accountability for overall faculty performance. But in recent years, as evaluation processes became a higher priority, the focus has narrowed to systems of teaching accountability, rather than on other aspects of faculty performance. Why the shift? Perhaps it is the result of the growing chorus of complaints from those who serve on promotion and tenure review committees that they are given little factual information about teaching performance. They argue that the typical curriculum vitae describes publications, research grants and other scholarly accomplishments but says very little about teaching.

It is no surprise that committee members are pressing for improvement in systems of teaching accountability. Without meaningful information about teaching, they argue, how can they be expected to judge a professor's performance? And how can they give the teaching function its rightful value?

The question is, can colleges and universities respond simultaneously to the state-of-the-art understandings about effective teaching and to the pressures to improve systems of teaching accountability? The answer is yes. A solution can be found by looking outside higher education.

PORTFOLIOS

Those in other professions—artists, photographers, architects—have portfolios in which they display their best work. These portfolios glisten with professional strengths. The portfolio concept can be adapted to higher education. A teaching portfolio would enable faculty members to display their teaching accomplishments for examination by others. And, in the process, it would contribute both to sound personnel decisions and to the professional development of individual faculty members.

At bottom, says Edgerton (1991, p.3) a portfolio would do what no other form of evaluation can do. It would "...enable faculty to document and display their teaching in a way that stays connected to the particular situations in which their teaching occurred."

Exactly what is a teaching portfolio? It is a factual description of a professor's major strengths and teaching achievements. It describes documents and materials which collectively suggest the scope and quality of a professor's teaching performance. It is to teaching what lists of publications, grants and honors are to research and scholarship.

For what purpose might a teaching portfolio be prepared? It can be used: (1) to gather and present hard evidence and specific data about teaching effectiveness for those who judge performance; and/or (2) to provide the needed structure for self-reflection about which areas of teaching performance need improvement (Pascal and Wilburn,

1978; Shore and others, 1986; Shulman, 1989b). It is vital to bear in mind that the purpose for which the portfolio is to be used determines what is to be included and how it is to be arranged. This point will be discussed in detail later.

The teaching portfolio makes no pretense to be an exhaustive compilation of all the documents and materials that bear on teaching performance. Rather, it presents selected information on teaching activities and solid evidence of their effectiveness. Just as statements in a curriculum vitae should be supported by convincing evidence (published papers or the actual research data), so claims in the teaching portfolio should be supported by firm empirical evidence.

2

PREPARING THE
TEACHING PORTFOLIO

PREPARATION

In theory, a teaching portfolio can be prepared by the professor working alone, but this isolated approach has limited prospects for improving classroom performance or contributing to personnel decisions. The reason, according to Bird (1989), is because portfolio entries prepared by the professor working alone enlist none of the collegial or supervisory support needed in a program of teaching improvement. It also provides none of the control or corroboration of evidence that may be needed to sustain personnel decisions.

In practice, the teaching portfolio is best prepared in consultation with others. A department chair, a colleague or a teaching improvement specialist on campus can discuss with the professor such important questions as: (1) why they are preparing the portfolio; (2) what they hope to learn from it; (3) which areas of the teaching-learning process they expect to examine; (4) what kinds of information they expect to collect; (5) how the information can be analyzed and presented.

Some may argue that the portfolio contents will be colored by second–party assistance and therefore is less useful because it represents "coached" performance. But Shulman (1988) disposes with this objection by arguing that portfolio development *should* involve interaction and mentoring in the same way that a doctoral dissertation reflects both the efforts of the candidate and the advice of the advisor. The solution to the so-called problem of coaching, he says, is to turn it around and treat it as a virtue. Agreeing, Bird (1989), suggests that joint production of portfolio entries may turn out to have the most formative value as well as assuring the relevance of the portfolio material to future personnel decisions.

There can be no doubt that preparing and reviewing teaching portfolios requires sound, informed judgment. For that reason, Seldin (1989) contends that department chairs, colleagues, teaching improvement specialists and evaluators need appropriate training to assure that they are qualified for their roles.

Professors, too, must learn how to study their own teaching and offer significant information about its effectiveness. They also need ready access to an organized collection of documents and materials used in previous portfolios, if available, and the written procedures that are applicable to many disciplines.

The resources of a portfolio consultant blessed with wide knowledge of current instruments and procedures to document effective teaching is especially helpful. The consultant needs to be familiar with, and have examples of, multiple approaches and techniques to demonstrate teaching effectiveness. In this way, the consultant can assist the faculty member by providing suggestions and resources, and maintaining support during the preparation of the portfolio. At the same time, the consultant instructs the faculty member how to select and use valid teaching records comparable to the records now kept for research and service.

KEY ROLE OF THE DEPARTMENT CHAIR

Shore and others (1986) point out that a teaching portfolio will have genuine value only when personnel decision-makers and faculty members learn to trust the approach. Important to the development of trust is the periodic exchange of views between department chair and professor about teaching responsibilities, duties ancillary to teaching, and specific items for the portfolio.

Seldin (1987) suggests that the discussion between department chair and professor should address expectations and how teaching performance is to be reported. Otherwise, he says, there is a danger that the department chair may erroneously conclude that the data submitted overlook areas of prime concern and may even cover up areas of suspected weakness. This possible misunderstanding is largely eliminated by an open discussion, especially when accompanied by an exchange of clarifying memos. When used in this way, the teaching portfolio attains the status of an important, trusted instrument. It provides the kind of flexibility and range of options that makes it adaptable to many units of the institution.

STEPS TO CREATE A TEACHING PORTFOLIO

To be useful, a teaching portfolio must include five key steps. These are compiled from the work of Seldin (1980), Shore and others (1986), Seldin (1987), and Vavrus and Calfee (1988):

Step 1: Summarize Teaching Responsibilites. Portfolios often begin with a statement concerning any agreement, formal or informal, between the professor and department chair concerning teaching responsibilities and criteria for teaching success. Try to summarize it in no more than two or three paragraphs. It might cover such items as number and types of courses to be taught, how students are to be evaluated, and the kind of progress expected by students. (In the absence of such agreement, the professor should include a brief statement on assumptions concerning teaching responsibilities.)

Step 2: Select Criteria for Effective Teaching. Bearing in mind the statement of teaching responsibilities in step one, the professor selects those items for inclusion in the portfolio which are most applicable to those teaching responsibilities. A factual statement about the professor's accomplishments in each area is then prepared. It is important that items chosen for the portfolio reflect the professor's personal preferences and teaching style. The goal is for individual professors both to itemize their teaching accomplishments and their reflections on their teaching to create a personalized portfolio.

Step 3: Arrange the Criteria in Order. The sequence of the statements about accomplishments in each area is determined by their intended use. For example, if the professor wishes to demonstrate teaching improvement, entries that reflect that goal (such as participating in seminars and workshops designed to enhance classroom performance) would be emphasized. Paragraphs or bullets help organize the statements, with extra space and attention devoted to those statements the professor accords major significance.

Step 4: Assemble the Support Data. Supportive evidence for items referred to in the portfolio should be safeguarded by the professor. Included might be such things as student workbooks or logs, journals on improving teaching, original student evaluations of teaching, invitations to contribute articles on improving teaching performance. The professor should give written assurance in the portfolio that such support data are available for review upon request.

Step 5: Incorporate the Portfolio Into the Curriculum Vitae. The teaching portfolio is then inserted into the professor's curriculum vitae under the heading of "teaching." The intent is to provide a record of teaching accomplishments so they can be accorded their proper weight with other aspects of a professor's role.

How much evidence is needed to represent equitably the professor's teaching performance? There is no simple answer. Knapper (1978) believes that the portfolio should not exceed three pages. Seldin (1987) suggests five to seven pages should be sufficient. Vavrus and Calfee (1988) point out that the professor must set the balance scale between "not enough" and "too much." Who can argue with that?

Before its preparation, it might appear that putting together a teaching portfolio would take more time than teaching itself. In practice, this has not proved to be the case. As preparation of the portfolio becomes routine and faculty members gain experience and skills, portfolio preparation wins an accepted place in institutional life. Generally, professors appear willing to invest time in an evaluation process over which they have some control (Berquist and Phillips, 1977; Seldin, 1987). If professors know that their teaching portfolios will be carefully scrutinized by tenure and promotion committees, it stands to reason that they will take greater pains to collect material along the way and develop the portfolios in the years prior to personnel decisions.

3

ITEMS THAT MIGHT BE INCLUDED IN THE PORTFOLIO

T he following list is *not* composed of items a professor *must* include. Rather, it lists the many possibilities from which the professor can select items relevant to his or her particular teaching situation. To some degree, the items chosen depend on the purpose for which the portfolio is prepared (improvement or personnel decision).

Since the portfolio is a highly personalized product, like a fingerprint no two are exactly alike. The content and the organization differ widely from one professor to another.

A word of caution. All college professors have seen poor student work dressed in fancy covers. The point of the teaching portfolio is not a fancy cover. Instead, it is a careful, thoughtful compilation of documents and materials that make the best case for the professor's teaching effectiveness.

This list of possible items for inclusion in a teaching portfolio is compiled from the work of Shore and others (1986), Sorcinelli (1986), Seldin (1990), and Bird (1989). These items are conveniently cross-referenced with the sample portfolios detailed in Chapter Eight. Please note the varying importance assigned by different professors to different items. Some professors discuss an item at length while other professors address the same item with just a sentence or two, or even omit it. Each teaching portfolio is a different, individual document.

MATERIAL FROM ONESELF

(1) Statement of teaching responsibilities, including specific

courses, and a brief description of the way each course was taught. (See all sample portfolios.)

(2) A reflective statement by the professor describing personal teaching philosophy, strategies, and objectives. (See all sample portfolios.)

(3) A personal statement by the professor describing teaching goals for the next five years. (See portfolios by Annis, Buckrop, Corso, and Riegle.)

(4) Representative course syllabi which detail course content and objectives, teaching methods, readings, homework assignments, student evaluation procedures as well as a reflective statement as to why the class was so constructed. (See portfolios by Annis, Bloom, Buckrop, Corso, Hodlofski, Ober, and Shackelford.)

(5) Description of steps taken to evaluate and improve one's teaching. This might include changes resulting from self-evaluation, time spent reading journals on improving teaching, participation in seminars, workshops and professional meetings on improving teaching, and obtaining instructional development grants. (See portfolios by Annis, Buckrop, Hodlofski, and Shackelford.)

(6) Description of curricular revisions, including new course projects, materials, class assignments or other activities. (See portfolios by Hodlofski and Riegle.)

(7) Self-evaluation by the professor. This would include not only a personal assessment of teaching-related activities but also an explanation of any contradictory or unclear documents or materials in the teaching portfolio.

(8) Contributing to, or editing, a professional journal on teaching the professor's discipline. (See portfolio by Shackelford.)

(9) Information about direction/supervision of honors, graduate theses, and research group activities. (See portfolios by Bloom and Buckrop.)

MATERIAL FROM OTHERS

(10) Statements from colleagues who have observed the professor in the classroom as members of a teaching team or independent observers. (See portfolios by Annis, Bloom, Buckrop, Corso, and Hodlofski.)

(11) Statements from colleagues who have systematically reviewed the professor's classroom materials, the course syllabi, assignments, testing and grading practices, text selection, and reading list. (See portfolios by Annis, Bloom, and Buckrop.)

(12) Statements from colleagues who have systematically reviewed the professor's out-of-class activities such as instructional and curricular development, and instructional research.

(13) Student course and teaching evaluation data which suggest improvements or produce an overall rating of effectiveness or satisfaction. (See all portfolios.)

(14) A statement by a chairperson assessing the professor's teaching contribution to the department and discussing how the department plans to use the professor as a teacher in the future. (See portfolios by Bloom and Buckrop.)

(15) Information on the professor's performance as a faculty advisor. This would come primarily from students, but supplementary information might also come from the department chairperson or advising coordinator or even from colleagues. (See portfolios by Ober and Shackelford.)

(16) Honors or other recognition from colleagues such as a distinguished teaching award or election to a committee on teaching. (See portfolios by Riegle and Shackelford.)

(17) Invitations to teach from outside agencies, to present a paper at a conference on teaching one's discipline or on teaching in general, or to participate in a media interview on a successful teaching method. (See portfolios by Buckrop and Shackelford.)

(18) Invitations to other campuses to demonstrate effective instructional methods, or to participate in teaching/learning symposia.

(19) A professional exchange with colleagues inside or outside the institution. The exchange might focus on course materials, or methods of teaching particular topics, or helping colleagues improve their teaching. (See portfolios by Annis, Ober, and Shackelford.)

(20) Participation in local, regional, state or national activities related to teaching courses in the professor's discipline. (See portfolios by Buckrop, Ober, and Shackelford.)

(21) Documentation of teaching/development activity through the campus office for teaching and learning. (See portfolios by

Buckrop, Corso, Hodlofski, Ober, and Shackelford.)

(22) Involvement in research that contributes directly to teaching.

(23) A full-period audio or videotape of the professor teaching a typical class. (See portfolios by Annis and Hodlofski.)

THE PRODUCTS OF GOOD TEACHING

(24) Student scores on professor-made or standardized tests, possibly before and after a course, as evidence of student learning. (See portfolios by Annis, Bloom, and Buckrop.)

(25) Student essays, creative work, field-work reports, laboratory workbooks or logs and student publications on course-related work. (See portfolios by Corso, Hodlofski, and Shackelford.)

(26) Information about the effect of the professor's courses on student career choices or help given by the professor to secure student employment. (See portfolio by Bloom.)

(27) A record of students who succeed in advanced courses of study in the field. (See portfolio by Bloom.)

(28) Statements by alumni on the quality of instruction. (See portfolios by Annis and Bloom.)

(29) Student publications or conference presentations on course-related work. (See portfolios by Hodlofski, Ober, and Shackelford.)

(30) Examples of graded student essays showing excellent, average, and poor work along with the professor's comments as to why they were so graded. (See portfolio by Corso.)

4

USES OF THE PORTFOLIO

PERSONNEL DECISIONS

Some argue that professors should be given unrestricted freedom to select the items best reflecting their performance. This approach may work reasonably well if the portfolio is used for improving performance. But it works less well if the portfolio is used for personnel decisions. Because each portfolio is unique, the lack of standardization makes comparability impossible for professors from different teaching contexts.

One answer, perhaps, is to require portfolios being used for tenure and promotion decisions to include certain mandated items along with elective ones. Such mandated items might include, for example, a reflective statement on the professor's teaching, summaries of student evaluations, representative course syllabi, and the chair's assessment of the professor's teaching contributions to the department. All additional items included in the teaching portfolio would be selected by individual professors.

Receiving Credit for Teaching Effectiveness

Although candidates for promotion or tenure may seek credit for effective teaching, usually only scraps of such information are available. The result is that the professor's teaching is often neglected in favor of research and scholarship where data are generally more plentiful.

Thus, professors wishing to receive recognition for teaching effectiveness stand to benefit by providing evaluation committees with their teaching portfolio. It provides the evaluators with the evidence upon which to make judgments about teaching performance.

The portfolio offers hard-to-ignore information to evaluators. It provides more than a compilation of student ratings. If certain items in the portfolio are standardized, comparison of teaching performance (five faculty members seeking promotion to full professor, for example) becomes possible.

Through the portfolio, the professor can add information about successful teaching to the portfolio of accomplishments in other areas. The portfolio will not grow indefinitely; like a publication list, it will be selective.

It is important to remember that use of the portfolio for personnel decisions is occasional. Its primary use is to improve the professor's teaching performance.

IMPROVING TEACHING PERFORMANCE

Can the teaching portfolio help the professor to appraise the quality of teaching performance? Seldin (1989) says yes. He points out that the portfolio enables the professor to: 1) ponder personal teaching activities, 2) organize priorities, 3) rethink teaching strategies, and 4) plan for the future. Properly developed, the portfolio is a valuable aid for professional development activities.

Just as students need feedback to correct errors, faculty members need factual and philosophical data to improve teaching performance. Feedback from a range of sources can produce in the teacher the kind of dissonance or dissatisfaction that sets the psychological stage for change. The portfolio can be a particularly effective tool for instructional improvement because it is grounded in discipline-related pedagogy. That is, the focus is on teaching a particular subject to a particular set of students at a particular point in time.

Whether such improvement actually takes place depends in large measure on the kind of information that turns up in the portfolio. It won't work unless the instructional elements to be strengthened are specifically singled out.

When used for improvement purposes, the teaching portfolio includes no required items. Instead, it contains only items chosen by the professor. For example, the professor might decide to improve one particular course and might include such items as: (1) a summary of instructional methods used, (2) specific course objectives, (3) the degree of student achievement of those objectives, (4) innovative practices, or (5) student ratings of course and instructor. Especially for new faculty, it is essential to pinpoint a specific area for teaching improvement.

One item in a portfolio used for teaching improvement might be a *reflective log*, according to Shulman (1989b). It would contain the professor's narrative responses to questions such as: What are you learning about yourself as a teacher? What is your opinion about something you learned? How might this new information help you in your teaching career now and in the future?

If the teaching portfolio is to stimulate teaching improvement, it must have multiple items and the data must be detailed, thoughtful, and diagnostic. Improved performance occurs when the professor is motivated to improve and knows how to improve. One thing is clear: few professors are able to improve their teaching performance without the help of others. Better performance is a more likely result if the professors discuss the portfolio items with a sympathetic and knowledgeable colleague or a teaching-improvement specialist. Professors, like everyone else, need reassurance that their shortcomings are neither unusual nor insurmountable; they can also use wise counsel in overcoming them.

OUTSTANDING TEACHING AWARDS OR MERIT PAY

Teaching portfolios can also be used to determine winners of awards for outstanding teaching or for merit pay consideration. One approach might be to encourage any faculty member who wishes to apply for an award or for merit pay to do so. Applicants would be required to submit their teaching portfolio.

OBTAINING A DIFFERENT POSITION

Applicants for faculty positions could submit their portfolios prior to an interview. Such a process would enable the applicants to highlight their teaching credentials and the institutions to assess the match between the applicant and the instructional needs of the college or university.

5

SUMMARY OF ELEMENTS IN THE PORTFOLIO

A dding a teaching portfolio to a curriculum vitae generally flags an administrator's attention because it fills the large gaps in teaching information needed for tenure and promotion decisions. Consider the following summary of elements in a sample teaching portfolio prepared by a professor who is to be considered for tenure. The examples given below are intentionally general since actual circumstances vary so widely. Items marked with an asterisk (*) are mandated for personnel decisions at this professor's institution.

TEACHING PORTFOLIO
Robert W. Harper
Department of Literature and Communications

Statement of Teaching Responsibilities*

Following a discussion, my department chair and I exchanged memos on our agreement about my teaching responsibilities. A year ago I gave up an introductory composition course, which I had taught for several years, and began an elective seminar in advanced writing. A student term project involving field-work and library research is part of that elective course. I also teach a required course in speech communication and an elective course in creative writing. I judge the performance of students in speech communication largely on in-class presentations. Students in creative writing are judged on language and dramatic development in their writing. I also serve as academic advisor to about 20 communications majors.

Personal Reflective Statement*

The appendix contains a personal, reflective statement about what I teach and why I teach it the way I do. It also has a discussion of my teaching contributions to the department and my teaching plans for the next few years.

Syllabi for All Courses Taught*

The appendix contains copies of syllabi for all my current courses. The syllabi describe course content and objectives, reading assignments, and student evaluation procedures.

Summaries of Student Course Evaluations*

In each current course, student satisfaction continues to exceed 3.90 on a 5-point scale. Over three consecutive terms, the rating in my advanced writing seminar has averaged 4.20. It has averaged 3.95 in my speech communication course and 4.35 in my creative writing course.

Elective Items

I am going beyond the mandated items and including a few additional ones since I believe they offer further insight into my teaching performance.

(1) Advanced Writing Seminar (Communications 420)

- An observation report on my teaching written by my colleague Professor Paul Gitelson who has observed me teaching this course three times in the past year.
- Four unsolicited letters by students.
- An instructional development grant award letter from the Teaching Resource Center enabling me to attend an off-campus workshop on teaching advanced writing.

(2) Speech Communication (Communications 216)

- A videotape of my teaching made by the Audio/Visual Department.
- Three unsolicited letters from alumni stating how the course helped them make effective on-the-job presentations.

(3) Creative Writing (Communications 295)
- A statement assessing my teaching from Professor Mary Torres who reviewed my classroom materials, including syllabi, assignments, testing and grading practices and text selection.
- Six examples of graded student essays showing excellent, average, and poor work.
- A letter of invitation to discuss my approach to teaching creative writing at a summer workshop sponsored by the Association of Departments of Communication.
- A letter from Professor Albert Smith of State College asking me to help him prepare a set of field experience notebooks similar to those I use in my course.

Appendix

Copies of all appendix materials and other printed items referred to in the teaching portfolio are on file and are available upon request.

6

RESOURCES AND SOME
CLOSING THOUGHTS

INSTITUTIONAL IMPLEMENTATION

The teaching portfolio concept has gone well beyond the point of theoretical possibility. Today, increasingly more institutions—public and private, large and small—are emphasizing, nurturing, and rewarding teaching through portfolios. A sampling of these institutions follows.

At the *University of Maryland-University College*, portfolios are the backbone of the rigorous selection process to determine the winner of the coveted Excellence in Teaching Award. The selection committee examines a variety of teaching-related portfolio items, using a rating form to ensure a uniform review. For more information contact: Barbara Millis, Assistant Dean, Faculty Development, University of Maryland-University College, University Blvd. at Adelphi Rd., College Park, Maryland 20742.

Harvard University works with teaching assistants (TA's) to develop their teaching portfolios for two purposes: first, to strengthen their case as skilled teachers for the external job market; and second, to help decide which TA's to hire to teach sections of large core courses, especially where the TA's are just names to the course leaders. For more information contact: James Wilkinson, Director, Danforth Center for Teaching and Learning, Harvard University, Science Center 317-319, One Oxford Street, Cambridge, Massachusetts 02138.

At *New Community College of Baltimore (Maryland)*, the length of a faculty member's contract renewal is partly based on the teaching portfolio. Among required portfolio items are: 1) examples indicating a commitment to teaching; 2) examples showing how the faculty members integrate the subject matter with the outside experience of their students; and 3) how the teachers establish and maintain rapport with their students. For more information contact: Raymond Yannuzzi, Assistant to the Vice President for Academic Affairs, New Community College, 2901 Liberty Heights Avenue, Baltimore, Maryland 21215.

The *University of Nebraska-Lincoln*, Psychology Department, uses portfolios to improve the documentation and evaluation of teaching for purposes of merit salary increases. The result after one year: a number of excellent teachers have been rewarded for classroom practices that had previously gone unrecognized. Other teachers have undertaken new teaching efforts. For more information contact: Daniel Bernstein, Psychology Department, University of Nebraska-Lincoln, 209 Burnett Hall, Lincoln, Nebraska 68588.

Miami-Dade Community College recently began using portfolios in the decision-making process regarding tenure, promotion in rank, and awarding Endowed Teaching Chairs. For more information contact: Mardee Jenrette, Director, Teaching-Learning Project, Miami-Dade Community College, 300 N.E. 2nd Avenue, Miami, Florida 33132.

At *St. Norbert College (Wisconsin)*, for more than a decade teaching portfolios have helped faculty grow professionally and have been used for personnel decisions. Also, the portfolios play a role in the annual faculty performance review by division chairs, as well as in the selection of sabbatical award winners. New faculty are encouraged to build their portfolios. For more information contact: Kenneth Zahorski, Office of Faculty Development, St. Norbert College, De Pere, Wisconsin 54115.

The *University of Colorado-Boulder* employs portfolios as part of the selection process for the President's Teaching Scholars Program. Established as a presidential initiative, that program honors and rewards faculty excelling at teaching and cultivates teaching excellence throughout the university. For more information contact: Mary Ann Shea, President's Teaching Scholars Program Coordinator, University of Colorado, Norlin Library S436, Campus Box 360, Boulder, Colorado 80309.

Roberts Wesleyan College (New York) makes portfolios the cornerstone of a professional growth model for faculty development and evaluation. An ancillary result has been the dialogue on good teaching that portfolios have generated. For more information contact: Elvera Berry, Professor of Communication, Roberts Wesleyan College, 2301 Westside Drive, Rochester, New York 14624.

The *University of Pittsburgh* uses teaching portfolios in a university-wide distinguished teaching awards program. Portfolios are found to be effective in particularizing the uniqueness of each faculty member's teaching record and in providing a basis for comparison. For more information contact: Margaret Waterman, Director, Office of Faculty Development, 1701 Cathedral of Learning, University of Pittsburgh, Pittsburgh, Pennsylvania 15260.

Gordon College (Massachusetts) is experimenting with the idea of extending faculty growth contracts to include portfolios, in order to make the reward system more responsive to teaching. The plan is to assist individual faculty members to develop teaching strengths in specific directions. The approach is for senior faculty to act as trailblazers and create models for the use of others. For more information contact: Jonathan Raymond, Dean of the Faculty, Gordon College, Wenham, Massachusetts 01984.

Among other institutions using the teaching portfolio or an adaptation of it are: *Indiana University-Bloomington*, *McGill University (Canada)*, *University of Guelph (Canada)*, and the *University of West Florida*. Numerous other institutions are field-testing the portfolio.

GAINING ACCEPTANCE OF THE CONCEPT

The teaching portfolio concept holds formidable promise to raise individual and collective performance levels in the classroom. But at many institutions there is a disturbing xenophobia toward strangers bearing new ideas. The teaching portfolio is no exception. Some professors resist out of anxiety and a tinge of fear that somehow they are threatened. Some administrators resist because they do not want to upset the status quo. Prudence, therefore, dictates that the concept be discussed openly and candidly by professors and administrators.

If the portfolio concept is ultimately to be embraced, a climate of acceptance must first be created. One way to break ground might be to field-test the portfolio on a handful of prestigious professors. The fact that faculty leaders are willing to try the concept will not be lost on other professors. These test runs provide not only useful experience for professors and evaluation committees, but also lessen campus resistance to the concept.

It may require a year, even two, before program bugs are ironed out and acceptance is achieved. After that, it is important that professors and administrators know that the portfolio program itself will be under periodic evaluation, and to know what the follow-up procedures will be.

SUMMARY AND CONCLUSION

Equipped with hindsight and the benefit of experience, we have learned a good deal about teaching portfolios. We know that:

(1) When teaching portfolios are used, the reward system becomes more responsive to teaching.

(2) Portfolios can be fitted into current evaluation practices with virtually no disruption.

(3) Portfolios serve as a springboard to enhance teaching performance, and teaching improvement is more likely if the professor discusses the portfolio items with a sympathetic and knowledgeable colleague or teaching improvement specialist.

(4) Teaching portfolios are both a result and a process. In preparing portfolios, many professors seem to make instructional choices that enhance their teaching performance.

(5) Portfolios must be individualized and comprehensive.

(6) Portfolios must be selective. They are not intended as a total compilation of documents and materials supporting teaching performance.

(7) Portfolios must be manageable, and cost and time efficient.

(8) On-campus portfolio consultants—department chairs, colleagues or teaching improvement specialists—are helpful to most professors in deciding what to collect for what purpose (for personnel decision or improvement) and how to present it.

(9) Assertions made in the portfolios must be supported by empirical evidence as requested.

(10) To develop trust in the portfolio concept requires periodic discussion between department chair and professor on teaching responsibilities, on ancillary duties related to teaching, and on selection of portfolio items.

(11) Most portfolios are five to seven pages, but there is no "right" answer as to length. Each professor must find the proper balance between "not enough" and "too much" in selecting material.

(12) Both the content and organization of the teaching portfolio must be relevant to the professor's individual teaching situation and relevant to the purpose (personnel decision or improvement) of the portfolio. There can be no doubt that professors can benefit by a systematic review of their teaching; the teaching portfolio is an effective vehicle for doing so. But it does more than that. Most professors will probably find the main attraction of the teaching portfolio is the chance to describe their teaching strengths and accomplishments for the record. That will give them a leg up when evaluation committees examine the record for tenure and promotion decisions.

Whether used for improving performance or for personnel decisions, the teaching portfolio is filled with promise, and so deserves strong support from professors and administrators alike.

7

AFTERWORD

THE BALL STATE UNIVERSITY EXPERIENCE

Since the spring term, 1990, more than one hundred faculty members at Ball State University (Indiana) have volunteered to develop their teaching portfolios. They have prepared statements outlining their teaching philosophy, collected materials documenting their classroom performance, and worked one-on-one with a portfolio consultant in a project directed by the author. Some professors developed portfolios for the purpose of teaching improvement, others for personnel decisions. Although the original seed money for the project was provided by the American Association for Higher Education, the bulk of the funding has been provided by the university.

How did faculty who prepared portfolios sum up the experience? The following comments are typical:

"A very rewarding experience."

"Preparing a portfolio has improved my teaching."

"I gained a renewed sense of pride in being a teacher."

"My chances of being promoted have probably doubled."

"I could actually see where I needed improvement."

What has been learned from the project? Most importantly that the portfolio concept proved to be fundamentally sound. It emerged as a practical and immediately useful approach to the problem of documenting the professors' in-class performance. Beyond that, certain benchmarks in the preparation and use of teaching portfolios were learned.

Strong Administrative Backing. Top-level administrators must give their active support to the teaching portfolio concept. That means they must be publicly committed and must provide the necessary resources to the project. At Ball State University the vigor of administrative backing proved essential in persuading faculty to invest time in portfolio preparation.

Open Communication. The portfolio concept must be presented candidly, completely, and clearly to all faculty members. Any sugarcoating or obfuscation in the explanatory process or in its implementation virtually dooms the program to failure. At Ball State, the portfolio concept was explained and discussed in detail at a general meeting of department chairs, at department meetings, and at a comprehensive workshop attended by the one hundred faculty volunteers

Individual Differences. Some elbow room must be allowed for individual differences in portfolios. Styles of teaching differ. So do demands of disciplines. It is prudent to allow for individual differences so long as these differences are permissible to the department and the institution.

Need for Models. Professors must have ready access to portfolio models. These models enable the professors to understand how others have put together documents and materials reflective of their teaching performance. At Ball State University, it was found helpful to make available portfolio models of exemplary, satisfactory, and unsatisfactory quality.

Portfolio Consultant. The resources of a portfolio consultant with wide knowledge of evaluation instruments and procedures must be made available to faculty. The consultant serves as a mentor who makes suggestions, provides resources, and offers steady support. The consultant's role at Ball State was especially significant since the faculty came to the teaching portfolio with no prior experience with the concept.

Evaluating the Program. The portfolio program must be designed to include an internal feedback mechanism for purpose of regular review. As the Ball State project ended, every faculty participant and many top-level administrators were asked for their comments and suggestions. Many of their observations will be incorporated should the program be formally continued.

Beyond these benchmarks, the project pointed up something else: virtually all participating professors acknowledged that in the process of collecting documents and materials they were forced to rethink their teaching strategies and goals. They asked themselves *why* they do *what* they do in the classroom. That alone induced many faculty to engage colleagues in discussion about teaching and to sharpen their own classroom performance.

Lastly, many professors found participation so useful that they plan to continue to experiment with the teaching portfolio.

A final word of caution. From the experience at Ball State University and at other institutions, we know that the portfolio cannot gloss over terrible teaching. Why? Because the preparer cannot document effective teaching performance. The evidence is just not there. On the other hand, for an excellent teacher the portfolio offers an unmatched opportunity to document classroom practices that have previously gone unrecognized. What better first step to the rewarding of teaching excellence?

SAMPLE TEACHING PORTFOLIOS

This section is comprised of eight sample teaching portfolios from across disciplines. They have been prepared by faculty at Ball State University (Indiana). The appendix material referred to is part of the actual portfolios but, because of its cumbersome nature, it has not been included in the book.

The portfolios are arranged in alphabetical order and prepared by the following faculty members.

Linda F. Annis
Department of Educational Psychology

Gilbert L. Bloom
Department of Theatre

Jacquelyn J. Buckrop
Department of Speech Communication

Laura Corso
Department of Home Economics

Leo C. Hodlofski
Department of Foreign Languages

David R. Ober
Department of Physics & Astronomy

Pamela B. Riegle
Department of Management Science

Ray Shackelford
Department of Industry & Technology

TEACHING PORTFOLIO
Linda F. Annis
Department of Educational Psychology
Ball State University

Table of Contents

Statement of Teaching Responsibilities and Objectives

I often feel like the Educational Psychology Department's utility player because, unlike most other faculty members who concentrate their teaching efforts in one of the major areas of the department, I teach courses across all departmental areas. Currently I teach both undergraduate and graduate courses in the Human Growth and Development area (35-45 students in each section), the "Study Techniques for College Students" course in the Educational Psychology area (25-30 students in each section), and a graduate seminar in research methodology for the doctoral program in School Psychology (8-15 students in each seminar).

My major learning goals for students in my human growth and

Linda F. Annis is Professor of Educational Psychology and has been on the faculty of Ball State University for twenty-two years.

development courses include gaining knowledge and comprehension of the basic subject matter, since I teach an introductory-level course at both the undergraduate and graduate levels. I also expect students to demonstrate ability to analyze examples of actual human behavior and to be able to apply what they have learned in proposing solutions to problems in growth and development. Student progress toward these goals is measured by multiple-choice exams with questions specifically designed to be at the knowledge, comprehension, application, and analysis levels of cognitive knowledge. The assigned course paper requires students to work with children and adults of various ages to demonstrate concepts discussed in class, such as Piaget's conservation tasks. Then students are asked to describe and analyze what they have learned as it relates to the course.

Students in my study techniques course are provided with a wide array of study techniques and encouraged to apply the ones that work best for them in different learning situations. In addition to being tested about knowledge of the study strategies presented, students also complete the Survey of Study Habits and Attitudes (1967) at the beginning and end of the course. This instrument provides pre- and post-course measures to determine improvement in study habits and attitudes. The major accomplishment expected of doctoral students in the research methodology course is to write a research proposal that can be expanded later into a dissertation. These proposals are evaluated both by me and the other students in the course using the same criteria that would be used by members of their doctoral committee.

Syllabi, Reading Lists, Assignments, Exams, and Handouts from Courses Taught

Appendix A includes copies of my current syllabi for all the courses I teach. Each syllabus includes a weekly breakdown of course content and objectives, any instructional media to be used that week, and dates for assignments and tests, as well as a detailed description of how final grades will be determined and classroom organizational policies such as rules for make-up exams. Also included in Appendix B are representative course materials such as exams, sample observation paper assignments for the human growth and development courses, and the detailed instructions for the research proposal to be written in the research methodology seminar. I am particularly pleased with the research proposal directions which have been fine-tuned over the years. Students who follow these instructions carefully produce a quality dissertation proposal that is approved with few changes by most committees.

Description of Efforts to Improve My Teaching

I take enthusiastic advantage of the many opportunities available on this campus to improve my teaching. During the past two years I have attended eight presentations on various useful topics in the Ball State University Series on University Teaching sponsored by the Center for Teaching and Learning. I also have participated in the Midterm Teaching Evaluation Program, the Partners in Teaching Improvement project, and the very intensive Teaching Improvement Process (TIP) where I worked on a one-to-one basis with a trained consultant to improve my teaching of the study techniques course. Documentation, such as Certificates of Attendance, regarding my participation in these activities is contained in Appendix C.

Peer Evaluation of Both My Teaching and Teaching Materials

During the past two years I have invited two colleagues from within the Educational Psychology Department, two from other departments, and professional staff from the Center for Teaching and Learning to evaluate my teaching and teaching materials. They used the standardized forms for peer evaluation and classroom observation provided by Seldin (CHANGING PRACTICES IN FACULTY EVALUATION, 1984). The completed forms are available in Appendix D.

My average scores on a five-point scale (with 5 being high) for the three major areas of the "Peer Evaluation of Teaching Materials" form were 4.5 for "Course Organization," 4.0 for "Readings, Projects, and Laboratory Assignments," and 4.2 for "Exams and Grading." I had an overall rating of 4.1 on the 13 items of the "Classroom Observation Report." The specific suggestions for improvement centered around increasing the number and variety of teaching and learning activities I use. This is an area I plan to focus on in the future.

Student Teaching Evaluation Data
from All Courses Taught for the Past Year

One of my colleagues administers Teaching Analysis By Students (TABS) evaluation forms for me each semester to every class after the first exam and then again at the end of the course. TABS provides detailed information on seven basic areas essential to good teaching: stimulating student interest, involving students in class, class organization and instructor's presentation skills, achieving closure, listening and questioning skills, showing concern for students, and evaluation methods. By studying these data for each course early in the term, I can make changes as required to maximize student learning and attitudes toward the course. My post-TABS results are consistently above 5.8 on a 7-point scale for all seven areas of TABS. Documentation of TABS for several courses is provided in Appendix E.

Videotapes of My Instruction

In Appendix F, I am providing videotapes of two of my classes which are quite different in format. The human growth and development course is basically lecture and discussion, while the research methodology course is a seminar taught around a conference table. The videotapes, available with the other appendix materials, feature a split screen with one camera on the professor and the other on the students so that both points of view are recorded. The human growth and development tape was made earlier this term, and the research methodology tape was made during the fall semester two years ago.

Measures of Student Achievement

Data comparing student pre- and post-course scores on the Survey of Study Habits and Attitudes (1967) from the study techniques course are included in Appendix G. These data indicate that by the end of the course my students, as compared to control students not taking the course, greatly improved their study techniques. Specifically, my students demonstrated a statistically significant improvement in avoiding delay in getting to work, in using effective study methods, and in showing more approval of educational practices, as well as an overall improvement in study habits and attitudes. Also included in Appendix H are graded sample observation papers written by students for the human growth and development courses, and a selection of research proposals written for the research methodology course.

Other Evidence of Good Teaching

The final Appendix I contains a collection of materials which I believe offer additional insight into my performance as a teacher. These materials include unsolicited letters from students at the end of the course commenting on my instruction and letters from alumni, as long as 10 years after they were in my class, discussing my course as they remember it and its impact on their lives and careers. Other kinds of evidence provided are statements from colleagues on campus regarding my assistance in improving their courses, and reports from colleagues at other institutions reporting on their use of the instructional materials and ideas that I have shared with them.

Future Teaching Goals

As my knowledge of the teaching/learning process has expanded through my teaching experience and my reading in the field, I now see the need to improve my teaching in two major areas. First, I want to incorporate more group work and collaborative learning into my classes. I plan to do this next year by observing the classes of three colleagues who are excellent in working with groups. Also, I plan to read more about collaborative learning and to attend a workshop on this topic during the next academic year. My goal at the end of two academic years is to incorporate at least one kind of group learning exercise into three out of every four class sessions.

My second major teaching improvement goal is to expand my knowledge of educational technologies and their use in the classroom. I plan to attend a workshop entitled "Visualizing Your Presentation" sponsored by the Center for Teaching and Learning next year. The following summer I will enroll in a "Video Information System" workshop. My goal is to learn how to produce video and audio materials for my courses. By the end of two years, I plan to have developed three instructional modules for my Human Growth and Development course.

Appendices
Appendix A: Current Syllabi for All Courses I Teach
Appendix B: Representative Course Materials
Appendix C: Documentation for My Teaching Improvement Activities
Appendix D: "Peer Evaluation of Teaching Materials" and "Classroom Observation Report" Completed Forms
Appendix E: TABS Document
Appendix F: Videotapes of Two Courses
Appendix G: Pre- and Post-Course Scores on the Survey of Study Habits and Attitudes
Appendix H: Graded Sample Papers and Research Proposals Contributing to Teaching
Appendix I: Other Evidence of Good Teaching

TEACHING PORTFOLIO
Gilbert L. Bloom
Department of Theatre
Ball State University

Table of Contents

Statement of Teaching Responsibilities, Philosophy, and Strategies

As a member of the faculty of the Department of Theatre I have several responsibilities in the area of classroom teaching. Virtually every semester I teach one or more sections of Theatre 100 (Introduction to Theatre), the departmental course which satisfies the Fine Arts portion of the Humanities and Fine Arts Distribution Requirement in the university's program of General Studies. It is a general one-semester survey of the theatre, normally taught from an histori-

---

Gilbert L. Bloom is Professor of Theatre and has been on the faculty of Ball State University for twenty-nine years.

cal perspective and including requirements involving both the reading of dramatic literature and the attendance by the student at a minimum of one live theatrical performance (usually on campus). Sections range in size from approximately 30 to 200 students. The major responsibility for the teacher of this service course goes well beyond the simple imparting of factual information. It includes an attempt to arouse awareness of what comprises the art form in all its complexity, the place of the art form in society (both historically and in contemporary society), and how the art form reflects the society in a given era. Additionally, and perhaps most significantly, the teaching of this course attempts to create in the student an appreciation of the art of the theatre — to build, as it were, good will for the art of the theatre specifically and for the fine arts in general.

My primary responsibility in teaching courses designed primarily (although not exclusively) for majors and minors within the Department of Theatre lies in the area of the history of the theatre. In this area I now teach a series of three courses (there were four before the university moved from the quarter to the semester system): Theatre 317 (History of Theatre 1), Theatre 318 (History of Theatre 2), and Theatre 319 (Modern Theatre). The first of these covers the history of the theatre through the Elizabethan era; the second covers theatrical history from the Italian Renaissance through the 19th century; the third deals primarily with twentieth century theatre, albeit with a nod to the late nineteenth century antecedents of developments in this century. In each course the major movements and developments in theatre history are discussed, including but not limited to such areas as theatre architecture, scenic conventions, costuming, acting and directing. All of these courses are included in the 33 credit hour Core Curriculum required of all Theatre majors, whatever specialty/option each may choose to pursue. In addition one course is required of Theatre minors, and all three may be chosen under the Directed Electives section of the requirements for the Minor in Oral Interpretation. It is my purpose in these courses to provide the student with a sound foundation concerning the background of the art form from its Greek beginnings to the present day in order that societal, political and theatrical conditions under which the drama has been presented over the years may be understood. Knowledge of these historical perspectives and our theatrical heritage is essential to the under-standing of the dramatic literature itself and should also offer the student insight into how best to approach the preparation of theatrical presentations in the present day, whether the student is a prospective performer, designer, or technician. In addition to these courses required of all Theatre majors, I also teach an additional course in the history of the American theatre (Theatre 413) which has been required on one option in the Theatre major.

It should perhaps be noted here that although these four courses are designed primarily for majors in Theatre, they are elected with some frequency by students pursuing other majors, particularly in English and the Humanities. They are also sought with sufficient frequency by graduate students in other areas that graduate level equivalent course numbers are maintained in the listings to accommodate such requests, despite the fact that the Department of Theatre offers only undergraduate degrees.

In addition to teaching these courses in my primary area of expertise, I also teach on a regular basis two courses in the area of Stage Lighting: Theatre 326 (Fundamentals of Stage Lighting) and Theatre 426 (Stage Lighting Design). Theatre 326 is basically an introduction to the tools of stage lighting, including such areas as the physics of light, lighting hardware and instrumentation, and basic principles of approaching a lighting design problem. This course is required of all students on the Technical Theatre (Design) Option in the Theatre major, and is designed to give students a basic under-standing of the equipment and processes involved in lighting the stage. Often students from other disciplines, especially Telecommunications, are also enrolled in this course. Theatre 426 is a course involving the actual design of lighting for specific productions, both on paper and in actual practice should the individual student prove sufficiently talented in that area. In both courses considerable "hands on" experience with the practical aspects of implementing a lighting design and operating control equipment for actual productions is required of the student.

While these courses represent the vast majority of my classroom teaching responsibilities, I have also taught courses in acting, directing, scenic design, and stagecraft, and am frequently sought out by students to supervise individual projects undertaken on the less formal arranged basis, or to act as mentor/supervisor/advisor on non-credit acting, directing, and design projects. I am also called upon to critique student acting auditions and technical portfolios in their preparation stages. These are also teaching situations, often on a one-on-one basis, as, indeed, are segments of the rehearsal/production process. The teaching of theatre must extend beyond the classroom to practical applications of principles learned therein. As a teacher, I also take advantage of additional exciting opportunities in co-curricular production situations as both designer and director.

Representative Course Syllabi

Appendix A contains copies of current course syllabi for those courses to which I am regularly assigned: Theatre 100, Theatre 317, Theatre 318, Theatre 319, Theatre 413, Theatre 326, and Theatre 426. Each syllabus includes a day-by-day breakdown of course content, reading lists, examination schedules, descriptions of research and other written and practical assignments (including dates for their submission). They also contain descriptions of course objectives and a detailed indication of the weighting of individual assignments in the determination of the final grade. In addition, references to visual materials and other teaching aids to be employed with various assignments and/or classroom discussions are included.

Student Evaluations of Teaching

Appendix B contains summaries of student evaluations of my teaching as reflected by the consistent use of the Purdue Research Foundation "Instruction and Course Appraisal: The Cafeteria System." In addition to the individual summary sheets provided by the university's processing system, a summary sheet for each course or group of courses is included comparing scores over a three-year period. Examinations of the long-term summary sheets reveal consistently high marks for teaching skills and strategies, with, in some cases, improved scores over the three-year span. The omission of summary sheets for the spring semester of 1989 reflects the fact that I was on research leave for that term.

Records of Student Performances on Pre-Tests and Post-Tests

In the fall of 1988 I began a process of diagnostic pre-testing of students at the beginning of the Theatre 100 course to determine student knowledge of and attitudes toward the theatre prior to taking the course. These pre-tests revealed a very limited understanding and appreciation of the theatre on the part of the majority of students enrolled. This comes, indeed, as no surprise, given the fact that most Ball State students have had little exposure to live theatre before matriculating. Post-tests, in the form of regular course examinations and an attitude survey at the end of the course, revealed both a substantial increase in knowledge about the theatre and an improved attitude toward the theatre in general once the course had been completed. In addition, many of the responses to attendance at individual theatrical performances have indicated both a new appreciation of the theatre and a willingness (even, in some instances, an eagerness) to continue to attend the theatre after completion of the course. These responses indicate that, at least to some degree, the objectives of the course are being accomplished. Examples of course examinations and pre-test and attitude survey instruments are included in Appendix C, together with summaries of results.

Statements of Peer Evaluations of Classroom Teaching

Included in Appendix D are statements from two of my colleagues who observed my performances in the classroom on a minimum of two occasions and responded to those performances on a standard form. One set of responses involved my teaching of the General Studies course (Theatre 100), the other came from witnessing my teaching of one of the courses in Theatre History (Theatre 317). In both cases the responses were generally favorable. Both colleagues also discussed the classes with me personally and provided valuable suggestions for ways in which my teaching might be improved.

Statements of Peer Evaluations of Teaching Materials

Periodically I have submitted course syllabi to colleagues for input as to the course requirements, teaching strategies, and teaching materials employed. Appendix E contains statements on these materials from two colleagues, both of whom were generally complimentary, although each made some suggestions for changes.

Statements from Peer Observations of Rehearsals

As indicated above, the teaching of theatre must go beyond the classroom experience by putting into practice the principles learned in course work. A part of this co-curricular extension exists in the rehearsal situation for actual theatrical productions. I am directly involved in such co-curricular teaching since I normally direct at least one major production a year. Appendix F includes statements from two of my directing colleagues and one from a colleague in the area of technical theatre regarding my conduct and accomplishments during rehearsal periods for major productions over the last three years.

Statement from Departmental Chairperson

I have solicited a statement from my departmental chairperson regarding my contributions to the department as a faculty member. This statement is appended in Appendix G. Particular note should be taken of comments concerning not only classroom teaching, but also my work in the areas of curriculum and course development and, additionally, of the fact that I have been appointed by the chairperson as both Chairman of the Departmental Curriculum Committee and Primary Departmental Advisor for the Department of Theatre based upon my experience and expertise in these areas.

Statements from Students and Alumni

Appendix H contains unsolicited comments from both currently enrolled students and alumni attesting to the significance of my teaching. Comments are favorable.

Record of Students in Graduate Programs

Appendix I includes a listing of former students who have pursued advanced degrees following the completion of the Ball State degrees, together with an indication of their individual successes.

Record of Supervision of Graduate Degrees

Appendix J contains a four-year record of my participation in the supervision of students involved in graduate education at Ball State. During this time I have served as a cognate member of two committees for doctoral degree candidates, one in English and one in Music. I have also, prior to that time, served on several additional doctoral committees as an at-large member. Prior to the separation of the discipline of Speech Communication and Theatre into individual departments, I also served on a considerable number of committees of Master's Degree candidates and chaired a substantial number of these committees.

Record of Student Performance in Advanced Courses and Production Assignments

A substantial number of students who have experienced my course in Stage Lighting have gone on to not only do well in advanced design courses, but have also been given design assignments for individual plays presented as a part of the departmental production program and at Muncie Civic Theatre. A record of such students is included in Appendix K.

Record of Students in the Profession

Several of our graduates have gone on to graduate work at other institutions and, further, proceeded to work in the profession. Some are practicing actors, directors and designers, while others have chosen to continue their theatre work in the educational setting, either in secondary schools or at the college and university level. Appendix L contains a summary of these students and their accomplishments in their chosen realms of the theatrical profession as both practitioners and educators. In all cases these persons have been students in my classes in the history of theatre, and in many cases in acting, directing, and technical theatre courses as well.

Appendices

Appendix A: Six Representative Course Syllabi
Appendix B: Fourteen Student Evaluation Summaries
Appendix C: Testing Instruments and Results
Appendix D: Peer Evaluations: Teaching Performance
Appendix E: Peer Evaluations: Teaching Materials
Appendix F: Peer Evaluations: Rehearsal Observations
Appendix G: Chairperson's Statement

Appendix H: Student and Alumni Statements
Appendix I: Students in Graduate Programs
Appendix J: Graduate Degree Supervision
Appendix K: Advanced Student Performance Records
Appendix L: Students in the Profession

TEACHING PORTFOLIO
Jacquelyn J. Buckrop
Department of Speech Communication
Ball State University

Table of Contents

Statement of Teaching Responsibilities, Strategies and Objectives

As a contract faculty member in the Department of Speech Communication, my teaching is mandated by the constantly changing needs of the department. I currently teach Speech 210 and Speech 240. Speech 210 (Fundamentals of Public Communication), as a course whose primary focus is on oral communication, is an introductory public speaking course. Speech 210 is required of all undergraduates, as it is a core course of the university's General Studies requirement. There are usually 25 students in the faculty-taught sections of this course. Speech 240 (Introduction to Human Speech Communication) examines the complex dynamics of communication and places primary emphasis on the understanding and application of communication theory; it is a survey course of human communication principles. Speech 240 is required of departmental

Jacquelyn J. Buckrop is Instructor of Speech Communication and has been on the faculty of Ball State University for one year.

majors and minors and students in the School of Nursing, although the course is taken frequently by interested others from the College of Science and Humanities, the College of Business, and Teachers College. The class usually has 24-26 students per section. (Other courses taught at previous universities may be found in Appendix A.)

My major goals for both courses are many, but all of them emphasize the knowledge and skills necessary to be critical consumers of communication and effective, ethical producers of communication. Students are expected to demonstrate understanding of communication theory through class discussions and exams (essay and multiple choice), and students are expected to offer sound, critical evaluation of outside speakers, scholars, and applicable research materials. Specific assignments for each class are detailed in the course syllabi (Appendix B).

Both courses are taught with a variety of teaching methods and media. Discussion and lecture seem to lend themselves best to the goals for Speech 210, while lecture, discussion and collaborative learning exercises best serve Speech 240 and as such are employed with greater frequency. Through lecture and discussion, students are encouraged to apply subjects to their own lives and experiences. These applications are then shared as a means to achieve greater awareness of gender, racial, age, and cultural differences. The major accomplishment to be achieved by the Speech 210 student is a problem-cause-solution speech with a question and answer period following. The speech is graded according to predetermined criteria. For the Speech 240 students the course culminates in a research paper which clearly connects the relevance of communication to a topic of their choice or further explores a topic discussed in class.

Representative Course Syllabi

Appendix B contains copies of current course syllabi for those courses to which I have been assigned at Ball State University: Speech 210 and Speech 240. Each syllabus contains a day-by-day breakdown of course content, readings, examination schedules, descriptions of research, and written and oral assignments (including their due dates). Also included are course objectives, grading criteria and weighting for assignments, and general course policies.

Record of Student Evaluations of Teaching

Appendix C contains summaries of student evaluations of my teaching as reflected by the use of the Purdue Research Foundation's "Instruction and Course Appraisal: The Cafeteria System." Also included are student letters detailing their evaluation of my performance in the class, the class structure, and their overall impressions. These letters were solicited in the respect that an open invitation was made to all students to provide me with their comments beyond the cafeteria evaluation form. Letters were received after semester grades were distributed and were requested because of potential reliability factors involved with surveying small classes. As this is my first year at Ball State University, teaching evaluations from other universities are also included in Appendix C.

Record of Student Performances

I am implementing a pre-test and post-test in Speech 240 during Spring semester 1991. At the end of this semester, the results of the tests and what has been gained in their use will be discussed. At this point, the tests are provided in Appendix D. Also in this appendix are representative samples of written student assignments; an example of an "A", "C", and "F" paper are included along with my comments as to why the papers received their respective grades. Pre-tests and Post-tests, plus videos of student speeches for Speech 210, are also included.

Statements of Peer Evaluations
of Classroom Teaching and Materials

Appendix E contains statements from departmental colleagues who have observed my performance in the classroom. Comments to date focus on my performance in Speech 240 and on original class materials developed for that course. Also included are statements from former colleagues regarding my performance and contributions in earlier teaching positions.

Statement from Departmental Chairperson

Appendix F contains a statement from my departmental chairperson regarding my role in and contributions to the department.

Record of Supervision of Students in Graduate Degrees

Because I am one of the few department faculty eligible to serve as graduate faculty, I have frequent contact with graduate students. Therefore Appendix G includes a list of graduate committees on which I have served and the students and types of projects supervised.

Description of Efforts to Improve My Teaching

I have great enthusiasm and pride in my teaching, so I take every opportunity possible to improve my classroom performance. I frequently attend university presentations on teaching, such as those sponsored by the Center for Teaching and Learning. I attend both the National Speech Communication Association convention and the regional Central States Communication Association convention, where I have both presented and participated in panels, seminars and workshops. I make use of student and peer evaluations during the semester and at the conclusion of the semester. I also read educational texts and journals pertaining to the education of my field and the education of college-level students, including *Quarterly Journal of Speech, Communication Monographs, Communication Studies*, and *Communication Education*. Examples of materials developed for professional and curricular use and record of attendance are contained in Appendix H.

Goals for Next Five Years

As the needs of the department and university change, as the number of majors and minors served by the department continues to increase, and as developments in the field arise and grow, I anticipate changing my goals — perhaps even before they are realized. Nevertheless, I have several primary goals relating to my teaching which I hope to accomplish within the next five years.

1) The field of communication, although dating back centuries, is ever-changing and growing in popularity and importance. My goal is to remain up-to-date in the field's research so that I can incorporate it into my classes and balance the teaching of skills and theory.

2) I plan to develop courses which are more culturally oriented, that is, which include more references to cultural, gender, and age differences in communication.

3) I plan to develop a course which examines the communication needs, differences, and importance for the differently-abled.

4) I plan to increase the use of computers in my speaking, persuasion, and rhetorical criticism and theory courses so that students may be aided in achieving computer literacy.

5) I plan to instill in my students the idea that the field of communication is: a) respectable, b) vital, and c) not just for those who cannot make it in other areas. In other words, I hope to dispel many of the myths about the field and break down many of the stereotypes I have encountered both as a student and an instructor of communication.

Documentation of progress made toward these goals, such as pertinent research, sample syllabi, and lists of suggested competencies, is outlined in Appendix I.

Appendices

Appendix A: Description of Previous Courses Taught
Appendix B: Representative Course Syllabi
Appendix C: Record of Student Evaluations of Teaching
Appendix D: Record of Student Performance
Appendix E: Statements of Peer Evaluations of Teaching and Classroom Materials
Appendix F: Statement From Departmental Chairperson
Appendix G: Record of Supervision of Students in Graduate Programs
Appendix H: Documentation of Efforts to Improve Teaching
Appendix I: Record of Progress Toward Goals

TEACHING PORTFOLIO
Laura Corso
Fashion Merchandising
Department of Home Economics
Ball State University

Table of Contents
1) Statement of Teaching Responsibilities, Philosophy and Strategies
2) Syllabi and Handouts from Courses Taught
3) Teaching Goals for the Next Five Years
4) Description of Efforts to Improve Teaching
5) Evaluation of Classroom Teaching
6) Reflective Statement and Closing Comments
7) Appendices

Statement of Teaching Responsibilities, Philosophy and Strategies

I am responsible for teaching the Fashion Merchandising courses in the Department of Home Economics at Ball State University. Within the department, students interested in textiles and apparel may major in Fashion Design, Fashion Merchandising, or Housing and Home Furnishings. Although I work in concert with other teachers in the fashion area, I am responsible for almost all of the fashion merchandising classes. This means that I must be a generalist within a specific field. Each semester I teach the introductory courses, as well as many of the senior level elective courses which are offered.

As the new faculty member in the fashion area, I was charged with the responsibility of making recommendations for revising the existing fashion merchandising curriculum. I have made several major recommendations for change which are currently being reviewed in

---

Laura Corso is Assistant Professor of Home Economics and has been on the faculty of Ball State University for one year. Previously she taught for twelve years in the Marketing Department at Broward Community College in Fort Lauderdale, FL.

committee. I anticipate that these changes will be made by Fall, 1991.

Many of our graduates will seek employment in the retail industry, others will go into wholesaling and support services. No matter where they secure their future, I hope to instill in them an enthusiasm for this business. Not only do my students need to understand the body of knowledge associated with fashion, retail management, apparel manufacturing, and textiles, they also need to possess a high level of human relations skills.

Therefore, as I teach the "material," I also teach the "feelings" of this business. Many of my students are currently employed or have been in some type of entry-level position within the industry. As a result, they can relate to the reality-based approach that I like to take in the classroom. In fact, I periodically take time off from my academic position to work in industry in order to insure that what I talk about in the classroom is indeed what is happening "in the real world."

The truth of the matter is that many students select Fashion Merchandising as their major based on false assumptions. I feel that it is my responsibility to help them to analyze these assumptions and assess their validity. This inevitably leads to some degree of fallout, but ultimately benefits the students in their long-term academic choices. The remaining fashion merchandising majors then collectively represent a much more committed group. There are positions available for every type of graduate, from the Merit Scholar to the student who performed marginally in the classroom but has the desire to make it work. I like to think that I am here to help all of these students find their niche in this business by exposing them to the information, helping them develop the competencies needed, and sharing with them my enthusiasm.

Syllabi and Handouts from Courses Taught
Appendix A: Course Syllabi

This appendix includes copies of my current syllabi for all courses I am teaching. Each syllabus includes the course objectives, a daily breakdown of course content, and the dates of any exams. Also, the attendance policy and grading scale are included.

Appendix B: Course Documentation

This appendix includes copies of exams, field trip observation forms, and selected assignments. Several of these need to be refined, which is something I hope to do now that I have survived my first semester at a new university.

Appendix C: Samples of Student Work

1) Two samples of student essay test questions from the first exam in HEMER 270, Fashion Industry, are included to show the standards used in evaluating freshman-level student essay responses.

2) A collection of materials used in HEMER 496, A Study of Fashion Designers, is included to demonstrate the method used in developing class research assignments and presentations. Two student research papers are included to show the appraisal technique utilized in this senior-level course.

3) A portfolio of representative student work completed Fall, 1990, shows the types of visual presentations resulting from the instruction in HEMER 345, Visual Merchandising.

Teaching Goals for the Next Five Years

In the next five years I hope to become more of a specialist within the field of fashion merchandising and retail management. Due to the nature of the Fashion Merchandising Program at Ball State University, it is vital that I have a thorough understanding of all areas related to the fashion industry. However, I would like to develop greater expertise in at least one of these areas. This focus will then provide foundation for the publications which are necessary for the promotion and tenure process. Therefore, I will begin work toward a doctoral degree in Retail Management at Purdue University. I am currently taking a graduate statistics course here at Ball State (EDPSY 641) which will be transferred to Purdue as I begin my program Fall, 1991.

I published a videotape last year to be used in the teaching of textiles. As a part of my endeavor to secure feedback on teaching materials, I asked the textiles specialist and the housing specialist to review the final product. Their comments were very helpful as I contemplate the production of other videos for classroom use. The owner of D.E. Visuals, the distributor of the previous videotape, has recently requested that I write and produce three additional videos

relating to visual merchandising concepts: color, the use of manne-
quins, and retail store fixturing.

Description of Efforts to Improve My Teaching

During my first semester at Ball State University, I have taken
advantage of several excellent teaching presentations relating to
improving classroom teaching. These seminars, offered by the Center
for Teaching and Learning, have been very thought-provoking and
helpful. In addition, I have attended workshops offered by various
departments to help build competencies in areas related to classroom
instruction, such as the use of specific computer software and the use
of our high-tech video system. I plan to continue attending as many
of these types of presentations as I can in the future.

Presentations/Seminars Attended:

1) Using Recent Research On Improving College Teaching &
   Learning
   August, 1990
2) Tips For Effective Planning Of Tests And Evaluation Of Student Achievement
   August, 1990
3) Teaching Portfolio Workshop
   September, 1990
4) Teaching Portfolio Conference
   October, 1990
5) VIS Seminar
   September, 1990
6) Open Forum With The Provost
   October, 1990
7) Computer Workshop: Lotus 123
   October, 1990
8) Rethinking What It Means To Be A Scholar
   November, 1990
9) Computerized Figure Analysis And Clothing Design
   November, 1990
10) Inventory Control: Knowing What To Buy
    November, 1990
11) Focus On Excellence: Creative Teaching Presenters Symposium
    November, 1990

Evaluation of Classroom Teaching

During the Fall, 1990, semester three of my colleagues observed my teaching on three separate occasions. An additional peer evaluation was completed Spring, 1991. On a five point scale, my peer evaluation averaged 4.93 for Fall, 1990, and 5.00 for Spring, 1991. The results were as follows:

Evaluator	Date	Class	Topic	Avg (5.0)
H. Steele	9/18/90	Fashion Industry	Lecture: "Textiles"	4.87
Comments: "Very enthusiastic lecturer." "Gave good reasons why students should know information."				
Dr. A. Finn	9/27/90	Visual Merchandising	Group Disc: "Loss Prevention"	5.00
Comments: "Very good relationship with the students." "Students all seemed very interested." "Nice job!"				
Dr. S. Whitaker (Dept. Chair)	10/1/90	Fashion Industry	Lecture: "Manufacturers of Apparel"	4.93
Comments: "A very nice job & you have a nice presentation style." "Good job with trying to get information out of them."				
Dr. J. Miller	2/12/91	Fashion Industry	Lecture: "Textiles"	5.00
Comments: "Extremely good use of questions." "Outstanding! What could be dry facts were presented in a very interesting way that stimulated student thinking."				

Student Evaluations

In my opinion, student evaluations play a very important role in assessing classroom activities. Following are the results of the student evaluations completed Fall, 1990. These evaluations include five core university questions, plus 35 questions selected by the instructor. A summary of the university core questions follows:

University Core Questions	Class #1		Class #2		Class #3	
Medians and Percentiles:	*Med.*	*%*	*Med.*	*%*	*Med.*	*%*
My instructor motivates me to do my best work.	4.5	82	4.8	96	4.9	99
My instructor explains difficult material clearly.	4.6	89	4.8	97	4.9	99
Course assignments are interesting and stimulating.	4.5	89	4.7	95	4.8	98
This course is among the best I have ever taken.	4.6	92	4.9	99	4.8	98
This instructor is among the best teachers I have known.	4.8	93	5.0	99	4.7	87

Student Comments

"I enjoyed this course very much. It helped me decide on a career path."

"I feel that Mrs. Corso is an asset to the department and is one of the best instructors I have ever had."

"I have learned more in this class than I have in my whole college experience. I have been waiting for a class like this one."

"This professor has had an exciting career and I am glad that I've had a chance to be a part of it."

"This class was a lot of work, but she was very encouraging and I enjoyed every minute of it!"

"This class has been an excellent learning experience. I have used so much of what I have learned already in my job in retail. Mrs. Corso is an awesome teacher; she really knows what she's talking about. This is definitely one of the best classes I have ever taken in this department and I'm looking forward to more!"

Copies of all peer and student evaluations can be found in Appendix D.

Reflective Statement and Closing Comments

As I reflect back over my teaching career of 17 years, I see tremendous growth on my part. I am hopeful that this growth is reflected in my classroom performance and that I am able to provide an atmosphere in which my students will be challenged, will be encouraged and, most importantly, will be successful. It is with much enthusiasm that I continue the process of improving my classroom teaching so that the true beneficiaries will be tomorrow's graduates.

Appendices

Appendix A: Current Syllabi/Course Outlines
Appendix B: Representative Course Materials
Appendix C: Samples of Student Work
Appendix D: Peer and Student Evaluation Materials

TEACHING PORTFOLIO
Leo C. Hodlofski
Department of Foreign Languages
Ball State University

Outline of Portfolio
1) Statement of Pedagogical Philosophy, Strategy and Implementation
2) Statement of Teaching Responsibilities
3) Summary Statement of Documentation
4) Appendices: Summary of Documentation

Statement of Pedagogical Philosophy, Strategy and Implementation

Teaching is an interactive process. More accurately teaching is one-half of a process. Teaching is incomplete without learning. Students willingly open themselves to a teacher's influence, but they retain all the qualities of any independent mind, including skepticism, judgment, resistance to new ideas, prejudices, false information, and pre-existing models of reality. In order to teach effectively, a teacher must learn the way in which the students understand and approach the material. For their part, students are not passive learners who simply absorb knowledge. They must be encouraged and motivated to participate actively in the process. My function as a teacher is to encourage growth in my students in two connected but distinct areas: I am the resource for introducing them to a specific body of knowledge; I am also the catalyst who can ignite an expansion in their critical thinking abilities.

My teaching methods are designed to support the dual goal of imparting an understanding of the content and encouraging growth in each individual student toward the next level of cognitive development. Assessing present levels of cognitive development, however,

---

Leo C. Hodlofski is Assistant Professor of Classics in the Foreign Languages Department at Ball State University and has been on the faculty for three years.

presents difficulties. I encourage students early in the course to express their interests and demonstrate their approach to course-related subject matter through an analysis of some items from contemporary video media. This presents content with which they are quite comfortable and upon which they are willing to comment. At the same time, I can use this opportunity to demonstrate that the subject matter which we are about to study is not as alien as it may have initially seemed, and that in fact they already have some understanding of the nature of the material. This classroom exercise provides a positive and enthusiastic initial contact and permits me to assess levels of cognitive development. It also provides a reference point for the students for the rest of the semester to which we can constantly refer to maintain a secure sense of where we are in the course, an especially useful tool when the material becomes more difficult and some students feel they are beginning to get lost in the details or in the more demanding areas of analysis.

For this process to be effective, students must be open to the teacher; but just as important, a teacher must be open to his students, to their view of the world, their approach to the material, their concerns, visions, fears and interests. From such a starting point, a teacher can lock onto the most effective means of connecting students to the material. The goal is not to reform the students in the teacher's image, but to give students new opportunities to grow in order to fulfill their own potential.

Structurally I divide the semester into several discrete units, each with a clearly defined content and structure, and each tied to an overarching theme which serves as the focus of investigation for the course (e.g., the growth of individualism; cultural values; the development of specialized knowledge; common cultural perceptions of self vs. other, of family, of individual development, etc.). This theme and the initial video discussion/reference point provide clear areas of focus for the course. Students can refer all assignments and lecture material to these foci and relate their work throughout the semester to a clearly defined and specific goal. (Language classes offer other difficulties concerning motivation and interest, but a clearly defined goal provides focus throughout the course.)

Yet every class presents a unique set of problems. The needs of freshmen are different from the needs of juniors and seniors. Freshmen approach material in an authoritative way, recognizing a right and wrong answer to a given problem and dividing issues into absolutes of black and white; upperclassmen focus more readily on process and evidence-based opinion. Pedagogical success depends upon a teacher's awareness of the different levels of cognitive development in his classroom and his ability to manipulate them.

Since every class is different, difficulties arise which require solutions particular to the needs of that class. The dual goals of imparting content and encouraging development of critical and analytical abilities are challenged most strenuously in classes with a broad mix of cognitive development stages. What works for one group might baffle another. If these levels can be recognized early in the semester, approaches to assignments can be adjusted. Offering options in each assignment is useful (e.g., analysis of an ancient Greek or Roman debate: "Which side of the dispute do you think is supported by the most convincing argument? Defend your choice with examples and explanation. What is the greatest weakness of this argument?"). Students respond at the level at which they currently operate. (Most juniors would consider nearly impossible an assignment to determine which side is correct, while a freshman would have great difficulty assessing the positive merits of both sides of the argument.) Offering options gives each student the opportunity to deal with the material at the level of his or her own development.

Challenging students to go beyond their current level of development presents the greatest difficulty. Maintaining the challenge and support necessary to encourage risk-taking behavior is difficult with a small class; a large class presents almost insurmountable obstacles. My pedagogical goal for the next two years is to learn and/or develop techniques for handling these problems in large classes. My current plan involves modifying what has been successful for me in smaller classes and applying techniques which colleagues have found successful.

Teaching Responsibilities

My primary teaching responsibility had centered on the General Studies courses which comprise 26 of the 34 courses taught by the Classical Culture faculty each semester. I am also now involved in the language area, teaching first and second year Greek, and in the soon-to-be implemented Classical Culture major, teaching the upper division requirements. This dual role, supporting the specialized major and minor requirements and the huge number of General Studies courses, is an interrelated responsibility. Most of our minors have been recruited from the General Studies courses, and so will our majors in all likelihood. Effective and exciting teaching is necessary in the General Studies courses; these, in fact, demand the greatest part of my attention because the huge amount of material covered in these courses requires intense organization and a clear sense of what is and is not possible on the introductory level.

In keeping with my concern for the quality of the General Studies courses, I have also worked closely with the members of the section who, with a Creative Teaching Grant, are developing a revised format for CC 105 (Greek and Roman Culture) which emphasizes the writing component. I have developed a pre-/post-test writing assessment instrument and evaluation criteria which can be applied consistently in any course with modification required only for the content portion of evaluation. Over the past summer, I coordinated the efforts of the section to revise CC 205 (World Mythology) to conform to the new syllabus approved by the Global Studies sub-committee of the General Studies Committee. We introduced a substantial writing component into the course. I also contributed to efforts to revise the third General Studies course, CC 101 (Word Origins and Vocabulary Development), to standardize the tests across the sections, reformat the workbooks, restructure the evaluation system, and resolve irregularities in the course's computer component.

Finally, teaching responsibilities must involve the teacher with students outside the classroom; being available for conferences and additional help, offering useful criticism on content and study and writing skills, and making oneself generally available for informal student interaction is the responsibility of every teacher who has ever complained that students fail to see the connection between the lessons of the classroom and life in the real world. Training students to be critical and analytical in their thinking cannot be restricted to the classroom; students who are engaged with the material eagerly search for ways to incorporate their new skills and knowledge into their lives. The teacher who takes the opportunity to assist in this kind of student growth gets the rare satisfaction of seeing the immediate effect of his efforts.

Summary Statement of Document

A. Summary of Student Evaluations (See full report in Appendix A)

1) Core items from representative courses using Purdue Cafeteria form; scale is from a low of 1 to a high score of 5:

CC 101 Word Origins and Vocabulary Development
CC 105 Greek and Roman Civilizations
CC 201 Greek Culture and Civilization
CC 205 Mythologies of the World
GRK 101 Beginning Ancient Greek
GRK 201 Intermediate Ancient Greek

GRK 101 (12 students reporting)
Fall 1990

Motivates Best Work	4.2
Explains Clearly	4.2
Assignments Interesting	3.5
Best Course	4.5
Best Instructor	4.6

CC 105 (16 students reporting)
Summer 1990

Motivates Best Work	4.7
Explains Clearly	4.7
Assignments Interesting	4.3
Best Course	4.5
Best Instructor	4.8

CC 105 (38 students reporting)
Spring 1990

Motivates Best Work	4.1
Explains Clearly	4.3
Assignments Interesting	4.0
Best Course	4.2
Best Instructor	4.8

CC 101 (37 students reporting)
Spring 1990

Motivates Best Work	4.2
Explains Clearly	4.4
Assignments Interesting	4.0
Best Course	3.9
Best Instructor	4.2

CC 101 (27 students reporting)
Spring 1990

Motivates Best Work	4.0
Explains Clearly	4.1
Assignments Interesting	4.0
Best Course	3.8
Best Instructor	4.0

CC 201 (6 students reporting)
Fall 1989

Motivates Best Work	4.8
Explains Clearly	4.5
Assignments Interesting	4.5
Best Course	4.5
Best Instructor	4.5

CC 205 (38 students reporting)
Fall 1989
    Motivates Best Work   4.3
    Explains Clearly   4.2
    Assignments Interesting 4.2
    Best Course   4.1
    Best Instructor   4.5

GRK 201 (4 students reporting)
Fall 1989
    Motivates Best Work   4.2
    Explains Clearly   4.8
    Assignments Interesting 4.2
    Best Course   4.5
    Best Instructor   5.0

CC 105 (41 students reporting)
Spring 1990
    Motivates Best Work   4.2
    Explains Clearly   4.4
    Assignments Interesting 3.9
    Best Course   3.9
    Best Instructor   4.5

CC 105 (10 students reporting)
Summer 1989
    Motivates Best Work   4.3
    Explains Clearly   4.5
    Assignments Interesting 4.3
    Best Course   4.0
    Best Instructor   4.7

2) Representative samples of student comments from the Purdue Cafeteria forms:

(a) "I enjoyed the emphasis on values. Congratulations on making me think! I know this sounds a little melodramatic, but you really have changed my entire outlook on life. Thanks for being the best professor at Ball State I've had so far!" (CC105)

(b) "Even though I probably did not receive the grade I'd like (B) I feel I learned more than in any class I have taken so far. You made us think and challenge our own values. This is something I would like to do in my teaching career." (CC105)

(c) "The only course and the only professor who has challenged me to think, work, question, and then some. Thanks." (CC105)

(d) "He seems to have a friendly openness to his ways. Eager to teach and help students as well. He is one of the most down-to-earth and realistic teachers I have ever known. I would like to take another course from him." (CC105)

(e) "Dr. Hodlofski does seem to know his mythology like the back of his hand. He encourages participation and has made me think in unique ways. Those students who do not do good participating are bound to fail. This is a hard class so you have to hit it home and never leave off. I enjoyed the class because I felt like I was part of a group think." (CC305)

(f) "Dr. Hodlofski is a great teacher. He presents material with enthusiasm and passion. I thoroughly enjoyed his lectures and his class. One of the best profs I have had." (CC105)

(g) "Dr. Hodlofski's class is the best I have taken in my 3 years at Ball State. I am going to recommend it to everyone I know." (CC205)

(h) "Dr. Hodlofski is an excellent teacher. I wish I had another year to take even more courses from him. His lectures are interesting and fun. Thank you for an excellent class." (CC105)

(i) "This course is very interesting and very relevant to other courses. Personally, I referred to this material in Old Testament, Anthropology-Women's Culture, and English courses. I appreciate the story-telling ability of the instructor and his comprehensive approach to such an important subject. It was a very worthwhile course. Thank you." (CC205)

B. Initiatives in Development of Course Syllabi

(1) Generated book of readings from 29 Greek and Latin authors for CC105 available through Kinko's.

(2) Created supplementary handout material on Greek and Roman political, social, cultural, archaeological, historical, and intellectual life for use in CC105.

(3) Initiated and directed the conversion of the CC101 Workbooks to Macintosh format for greater readability.

(4) Participated in rewriting of all testing materials for CC101 over the summer to have revised and newly formatted versions available at the beginning of Fall Semester 1990.

(5) Co-coordinator of CC205: supervised (a) implementation of revised syllabus which stresses greater inter-cultural analysis and (b) the inclusion of writing as a required part of the course.

(6) Created supplementary handout material for CC205 to assist students in mastering material not sufficiently covered in the textbook.

(7) Implemented substantial writing component into CC105 and CC205 in support of Writing Across the Curriculum Program. Assessed relative effectiveness of in-class assignments, non-graded assignments, exam assignments, and take-home assignments.

(8) Revised the writing components in upper division courses (CC201, 301 and 305) to stress the more technical aspects of research and writing.

C. Peer Evaluations (See full reports in Appendix C)

(1) Classroom observation, CC205 (World Mythologies), Dr. W. Magrath (20 Nov. 1990)

"A treat! Professor Hodlofski's chore was to deliver an interesting and informative lecture on 'death' to over 100 students in an introductory mythology course, and he did so with clarity, depth, and variety."

(2) Classroom observation, CC205, Dr. R. Gardiol (30 Oct. 1990)

"...instructor was well prepared. Lecture was well organized, presentation was made interesting by pertinent allusions."

(3) Classroom observation, CC205, Dr. E. Kadletz (11 Oct. 1989)

"His presentation was vivid and animated."

D. Efforts to Improve Teaching

(1) Under a program sponsored by the Center for Teaching and Learning (CTL) I had one of my lectures videotaped (CC205, Mythologies of the World, 20 Nov. 1990). I reviewed the tape with the Director of the CTL, Dr. Linda Annis. This proved to be a valuable experience of self-evaluation which made me more aware of such issues as my style and pace of delivery, physical movement and intonation, as well as the level of clarity in my lecture, amount of repetition and variety in presenting important points, and level of reliance on written notes. I received helpful advice and suggestions and a useful reading list of pedagogical analyses of ideas I hope to incorporate into my classes.

(2) I have prepared a teaching portfolio in consultation with Dr. Peter Seldin. I met him in the course of a General Workshop (6 Sept. 1990) and pursued the process in three meetings with Dr. Seldin (4 Oct. and 29 Nov. 1990, and 23 Jan. 1991). The process of generating the portfolio has been an enlightening one. It has been particularly helpful in improving my teaching by imposing on me the task of confronting my own teaching philosophy, style, and methods. Putting these into writing has been a challenging and reflective process during which I analyzed in detail the expectations and biases I take with me into the classroom, my goals and objectives on a course-specific level, my methods for achieving those goals and, not least, the reasons I chose a teaching profession. The clarity of purpose which has resulted from this process has been invigorating and, I believe, has had quite

tangible results in the classroom.

(3) I have attended the last six lectures sponsored by the Center for Teaching and Learning over the past year and a half. Topics:

"Learning in Groups," Dr. Richard Henak, 29 Jan. 1991;

"Rethinking What it Means to be a Scholar," Dr. R. Eugene Rice, 6 Nov. 1990;

"Who is in Class and How do They Develop?" Dr. Frances Lucas, 25 Sept. 1990;

"Effective Discussion Teaching: Lessons from the Case Method," Dr. William Welty, 27 March 1990;

"Teaching Values: Who Gets to Use the Chalk?" Dr. Lee Humphries, 30 Jan. 1990;

"Conducting Effective Classroom Discussion," Dr. Susan Ambrose, 7 Nov. 1989.

E. Student Outcomes

1. Research paper advisor for advanced undergraduate Ronald Meade whose refereed paper, "An Observation of Wrestling Techniques in Ancient Greece Through Its Art and Literature," was selected for presentation at the Kentucky Foreign Language Conference April 28, 1990.

2. Special Assignments and Independent Studies Supervision:

(a) Andonis Neophytou (CC498, Selected Topics in Greek Myth, Spring 1989)

(b) Ronald Meade (CC498, Selected Topics in Greek Culture, Spring 1990)

(c) Kevin Nolley (FL590, Independent Study: Exploration of Teaching Methods in Vocabulary Development, Summer 1990)

(d) Special tutoring in Greek: two students expressed interest in second semester Greek in the seventh week of Fall 1990 Semester. Since Greek 101 is necessary for Greek 102, students joined Greek 101 with the provision of meeting for an additional two to three hours per week with the instructor to cover the earlier material. Both successfully mastered the material and are doing superior work in Greek 102.

3. Samples of student essays and papers from General Studies courses and upper division Classical Culture courses.

Appendices: Summary of Documentation

Appendix A: Summaries of Student Course Evaluations
Contains: (1) A copy of student course evaluations during the past two and a half years. On a 5-point scale, my classes average in the 4 range, with rarely any individual item ratings below 4.0. Language classes receive especially superlative scores. (2) Copies of student comments from evaluation forms.

Appendix B: Syllabi for Courses Taught
Contains copies of syllabi for the courses I currently teach, including course descriptions, objectives, methods, assignments, and evaluation criteria.

Appendix C: Peer Review
Contains evaluation reports from (1) the Department Chair and (2) the Classics Section Coordinators who have observed my teaching in the past year.

Appendix D: Efforts to Improve Teaching
Contains documentation (1) of meetings with Dr. Linda Annis pertaining to a review of videotape of my lecture and (2) of attendance at seminars sponsored by the Center for Teaching and Learning.

Appendix E: Student Outcomes
Contains (1) copies of the program from the Kentucky Foreign Language Conference at which my student, Ronald Meade, presented a paper and (2) samples of student essays and papers from General Studies and upper division Classical Culture courses.

TEACHING PORTFOLIO
David R. Ober
Department of Physics and Astronomy
Ball State University

Table of Contents

Statement of Teaching Responsibilities

My academic-year teaching responsibilities include assignments with students at both the graduate and undergraduate levels. During the past several years I have taught and served as the departmental coordinator for a year-long introductory calculus-based general physics course (PHYCS 120, 122) taken by all departmental majors, minors, and pre-engineering students. In addition, I have taught specialty courses in physical optics, nuclear laboratory techniques, and nuclear physics for both upper division majors, minors, and graduate students. In these courses and as a designated departmental advisor of undergraduates, I counsel students in the areas of course selection and career opportunities.

The Department of Physics and Astronomy offers a wide variety of summer enrichment opportunities and updating/retraining courses for high ability high school students and high school teachers, respectively. These programs began in 1975 through a series of four

David R. Ober is Professor of Physics and Astronomy and has been on the faculty of Ball State University for twenty-three years.

grants from the National Science Foundation (NSF) as a part of the Student Science Training Program for high school students; in 1982 the department's teacher updating/retraining program was initiated utilizing a similar workshop format. The teacher program has grown to the level where during the summer of 1989 I was one of six Physics and Astronomy Department faculty members who instructed in ten separate workshops; in addition to this activity, another faculty member and I conducted the second year of an NSF grant program in electronics for the high school students. During the academic year I serve as coordinator for both the high school student and teacher summer programs.

Syllabi, Study Guides, Mini Notes, Laboratory Activities, and Exams for Courses Taught

The appendix contains syllabi and schedules for courses that I have taught in the past year. The course "information sheets" provide the students with a record of exam schedules, extra-credit options, and relative weighting of homework, laboratory, and exam scores for course grade determination. Also included in the appendix are representative chapter study guides and exams for the year-long beginning physics courses (PHYCS 120 and 122) that I have taught. Each chapter study guide provides a one- to three-page summary of objectives, skills, review list, and equations and concepts.

Examinations are designed to assess the student's problem solving skills; in my first-year beginning courses, each student is responsible for preparing his/her own "Equation Sheet" which may be used during the exam.

The mini-note/incomplete-note lecture format has been used extensively in the summer workshop programs for both the high school students and teachers. Hands-on laboratory experiences are an important component of both the academic-year and summer offerings. Representative mini-notes and laboratory experiments that I have developed for these courses are presented in the appendix.

Summaries of Course Evaluations by Students

Summaries of my academic-year course evaluations by students over the past six years are kept in the department chairman's office.

In each instance I have used the standard Ball State University Cafeteria System Evaluation form that is administered through the Evaluation/Scanning Services Office.

Evaluations always have been an important resource for improving and developing summer workshop programs for high school students and teachers. Complete summaries of these evaluations are on file in the department office.

Teaching Improvement Activities

The Ball State University Department of Physics and Astronomy has set a high priority on quality teaching. Therefore, faculty members continually work to develop and share with one another new demonstrations for lectures and new experiments for laboratory activities. I have been an active contributor and participant in this process through my attendance at state, regional, and national meetings of physics teacher organizations such as the American Association of Physics Teachers, American Physical Society, National Science Teachers Association, and Indiana Academy of Science.

In the fall of 1986, I was one of five Ball State University faculty members who were invited to take part in a two-day training session entitled "Teaching Improvement Process" (TIP). This program was sponsored by the University's Center for Teaching and Learning and it was designed to provide consultants for faculty who volunteered to participate in the program. Since that time, I have worked with 11 clients from eight departments of the College of Science and Humanities. Evaluations of my work in this program are on file at the Center for Teaching and Learning. Letters of appreciation from former clients are included in the appendix.

I believe that my students and I have benefited immensely from the TIP program. The TIP program has given me the opportunity to observe many excellent teachers throughout the university. I have assisted them by administering the Teaching Assessment by Students (TABS) evaluation instrument, and then interpreting the results of TABS. I also have worked with them in analyzing videotapes of their classroom lectures and, finally, in planning strategies for instructional improvement. These experiences have improved my own awareness of strategies in the teaching and learning process.

While working in the TIP program, I have administered the TABS instrument to my classes and my teaching has been videotaped. These materials are available upon request. The TIP program has permitted me to implement new teaching strategies in my classes. I continue to benefit from the experience of the other TIP teaching consultants and the director of the Center for Teaching and Learning as we work with new clients.

Undergraduate Fellows/
High School Summer Research Students

I have served as the advisor to an Honors College Undergraduate Fellow each of the past two years. In addition to contributing to a group research project, each Fellow has carried out a research project of his or her own and has presented a paper at a state professional meeting. Abstracts of these papers are presented in the appendix. I am currently serving as the undergraduate Honors Thesis advisor for a former Undergraduate Fellow who has remained with the project a second year.

Since the summer of 1984, our department has participated in the Research Engineering Apprenticeship Program (REAP) through a grant from the New Hampshire Academy of Applied Science. Each summer this program has brought to our department 10-15 high-ability high school students who have participated in four- to seven-week research experiences. I have served as the coordinator for this program and I have advised participants in nuclear research projects while other faculty members have advised projects in solar energy and astrophysics. The final reports prepared by the students taking part in these projects are on file in the department office.

Reflective Statement and Closing Comments

In the teaching/learning process, my primary aim is to create an environment and plan of study in which the student can be successful. It is important that the student experience successes at regular intervals; I arrange for this to occur through homework exercises, laboratory experiences, and optional extra-credit incentives. I attempt to design my courses in such a way that physics students will continually experience progress in a manner similar to that experienced by athletes and musicians through their daily practices. This must occur in an atmosphere of mutual respect, trust, and positive reinforcement. The TABS evaluation instrument used in the TIP program allows me to monitor student attitudes in these areas.

Finally, I want to convey to my students what physicists really do in their daily work. I attempt to accomplish this goal by relating physics to real-life situations. The majority of our summer courses for both high school students and teachers have been developed around applied physics themes; these have included such topics as lasers and holography, medical and environmental radiation applications, solar energy, and analog and digital electronics. Letters from former graduates and participants of our programs indicate that this philosophy has provided our students with an appreciation for the research aspects of our discipline and stimulated their creative abilities.

As we look forward to the next few years, one can be assured that educators will be challenged to meet society's ever-changing needs and demands. Accountability, assessment, and new technology in classroom delivery will remain as major opportunity areas for individual improvement. Personally I would like to develop alternative classroom delivery methods which will utilize a recently installed university Video Information System. Furthermore, in much the same way that we train our students through independent research/ laboratory activities, I would propose that students work side by side with their mentors in preparing these new instructional materials and delivery systems as part of their professional training. The current outlook for employment opportunities in academic positions is very optimistic. Each of us has the responsibility to assist in attracting top students into academic careers. In addition to gaining valuable skills in such teaching-related activities, one-on-one interactions with university staff members will be valuable career exploration experiences for students.

Appendices
Appendix A: PHYCS 120, 122, and 330 Course Syllabi

Appendix B: Representative Chapter Study Guides for PHYCS 120 and 122

Appendix C: Representative Examinations for PHYCS 120 and 122

Appendix D: Representative Mini-Notes and Laboratory Experiments
for Summer Programs
  • High-Ability High School Students
  • Secondary Teachers
Appendix E: Letters from Former TIP Clients
Appendix F: Abstracts of Research Papers Presented by Honors
College Fellows

TEACHING PORTFOLIO
Pamela B. Riegle
Department of Management Science
Ball State University

Table of Contents

Introduction
The purpose of my teaching portfolio is to force self-evaluation, to create additional feedback on my job performance, and hopefully to identify ways to improve.

As an instructor of management science, my role in the department is to fill-in as needed, covering those classes that are not covered by the tenured faculty. Because senior faculty members have their specialty areas, the classes I instruct most often are the basic introduction-level classes. This role gives me a unique and challenging platform for my teaching goals for the next five years.

Future Goals

Goal 1
My primary goal for the future is to take my introduction-level classes and make them my specialty, my area of expertise. Where frequently these classes become the filler to complete a teaching load

---

Pamela B. Riegle is Instructor of Management Science and has been on the faculty of Ball State University for four years.

for a professor and therefore low in priority behind an area of expertise, these classes are my primary objective, the full beneficiary of my preparation time and research.

As a means of reaching this goal, I must constantly update my teaching materials to give students the most current information possible. New, interesting examples that will make obscure management theories understandable and allow students to better relate are a must.

Goal 2

Because the classes I teach are foundations upon which higher level classes expound, I feel a great obligation to my students to make sure they are prepared to move on. Pursuing a greater level of retention of core knowledge is another goal. I want to go beyond a student completing the class with a passing grade. I want to achieve a level of familiarity with the core body of knowledge so it is comfortably retained for use in future classes and in life.

Goal 3

My students are consumers paying me to impart knowledge, to cause them to learn. When a student fails to learn, I fail. If my current methodology is not reaching the student, I need a new method. If the student is not motivated to attend class and learn, again I fail by not motivating, not corresponding the necessity or value of the knowledge I have to share. I intend to give my students (sometimes in spite of their actions) the product they have paid for: knowledge.

To this end, I hope to constantly improve the educational environment of my classroom. I will strive for more motivation to inquire, more efficient communication, a relaxed atmosphere that invites student involvement, and an environment that makes students think.

Goal 4

My goal with regard to my colleagues is to send them students, even poor performers, who are better informed, better prepared, and motivated to learn more about business.

Goal 5

I want not only to make my students business-wise, but also understanding of how they personally can and should fit into the world of business. I want them to be able to recognize their particular skills and talent and take an enthusiasm for business into their workplace.

Classroom Standards

The grade basis for my classes is a point system. This system allows the students constant feedback on their position in the class.

I have established tough standards of performance. I maintain attendance records and penalize points for unexcused absence. Because most of the information I provide in lecture cannot be gained by simply reading the text, students must be present to attain this knowledge. Also, I am establishing a standard for attendance that will be expected in higher-level classes and in the business world: show up and perform or lose.

I do not use multiple-choice or true/false style tests. Because the knowledge base I teach is fundamental to future classroom success, I feel it must be absorbed beyond the level necessary to complete the above mentioned test forms. Therefore, my tests are set up for short answer or essay. Detailed information is a must for total points. They must express both the "what" and the "why."

Individual Class Objectives and Activities

MGS 200: Introduction to Management

In this class, my main objective is to establish a foundation of knowledge on management in preparation for future business classes. Beyond learning the history and theories, I like to give my students the opportunity to test their management skills through the use of case analysis, research, group activities and individual presentations.

I am also aware that many of the students in this class are from outside the College of Business and have selected MGS 200 as an elective. For these students, this class may be their total exposure to business information.

To accommodate both varieties of student, I emphasize how management plays a role in their present life and in their future, even if they never become a manager in business. I truly believe much of the material presented in this class could benefit every college student.

For covering the individual topic of discussion, my lectures combine the textbook material with my own outside research. Frequently, the ancillary material will comprise as much as eighty percent of my lecture.

Sources for this additional material include current business periodical updates and real life examples to clarify and append textbook presentations. I view my role as an enhancer of the given materials, not a replay of the information students purchased in the text.

I feel that case study analysis is one of the best methods for conveying management knowledge. The student must put himself/herself in the role of the manager and solve the case problems based on sound management practices. I use this teaching tool for individual analysis and also as an exercise in small group interaction. The students get a feel for the role the manager plays and how the textbook knowledge fits into that role. I have MGS 200 students complete research at two levels. On a small scale, students are required to search current business periodicals for articles related to current class topics and they must prepare a formal presentation to the class expressing the crux of the article. The student experiences the managerial role of preparing and presenting information to an audience in a professional atmosphere. Additionally, the student is exposed to current business periodicals and frequently picks up much more information than is needed to fulfill the assignment.

On a deeper note, students are required to complete a term paper. The student is to interview a manager of their choice with queries of business-relevant topics. They have a list of mandatory interview questions about which they must be totally knowledgeable, such as strategic planning or job scope and depth, so they can maintain a professional atmosphere during the interview process. In addition, they are required to create their own questions for the interview to complete the minimum page requirements of the paper.

This assignment allows the student to hone both oral and written communication skills. Additionally, the student is presented with an opportunity to talk with an active business manager. (Appendix A)

MGS 221: Business Statistics

In addition to mandatory attendance and detailed testing, I am adamant about completion of homework in statistics. I check homework on a regular basis, not for correct answers, but for effort. Based on previous experience, I have found that what my students fondly refer to as my "blackmail tactics" of class attendance and homework completion makes for the greatest success level, a level that provides for success in future statistics-related courses.

I also set my grading scale higher in statistics. Because of the retention level necessary to continue in higher-level statistics classes, my students must have a minimum of 75% scoring to pass my class.

Examples of Course Enrichment

I frequently have the pleasure of having a number of non-traditional students in class. I view these students as a great resource. They have full-time jobs or at least more job experience than the traditional students. They have a wealth of examples and experiences from real life that lend meaning and credibility to textbook knowledge.

A lecture area I felt was weak in my presentation was the history chapter in Introduction to Management. The students viewed it simply as a list of names and dates to memorize. I felt there was a much bigger picture they were missing.

My solution was to create a time line dating from 1850 to the present. Next, I highlight major historical events such as wars. Then, I go back and place a few significant inventions, such as indoor plumbing, the telephone and the television, on the line to give a feel for the lifestyle of the given times. Then I put in place business-relevant historical events, such as major union movements and Henry Ford's $5.00 work day. Finally, I put on the people and dates presented in the text adding some personal facts researched on each, as well as about the person's philosophy or contribution, and each study becomes a product of its time.

I find this method of conveying this body of knowledge not only makes learning the names and dates easier, but they also gain a better perspective on the progressive nature of business activities and practices.

Measures of Teaching Effectiveness

Student Evaluation Results

My student evaluation scores, the only teaching ability evaluation criteria used in my department, are consistently high, above the department average. Below are the results for Fall Semester of 1989.

	Department Average	My Average
Teaching Ability	4.25	4.90
Professional Behavior	4.48	5.00
Overall Rating	4.31	5.05

As shown on the six-point scale, with three being average, my scores were consistently good.

Additionally, when questioned on whether the student would take a course from me again, 134 out of 136 students surveyed said they would. Of the two students who declined, one stated the grading scale was too high and the other student stated that the homework load was excessive. Both of these complaints I view as positive, not a reflection of poor teaching performance.

Below are examples of evaluation comments I feel convey the overall mood expressed on most of my student evaluation forms:
"Explains well"
"Prepared"
"Interesting"
"Knows the material"
"Communicates well, clear, concise, easily understood"
"Uses simple everyday examples to explain complex items"
"Gets us involved"
"Relates management to our own use and business"
"Relaxed manner, easier for students to talk"
"Methods are easily comprehended and clear"
"Relates well to students"
"Helpful, kind, available"
"Seems to have a genuine concern for all students"
"She makes you think"
(Appendix B)

Awards
I have been selected as a recipient of the 1989/1990 Dean's Outstanding Teacher Award. In order to qualify for consideration, a faculty member must teach full-time and rank in the top 25% of the department according to student evaluations. (Appendix C)

I have received additional recognition as one of Ball State's finest educators in the form of a student vote. Students were given the opportunity, as part of class registration, to vote for an instructor who had a positive impact on their academic career at Ball State. I was recognized as one of eighty instructors campus-wide to receive significant votes as a percentage of student's votes in each nominee's class. (Appendix D)

Rewards

I have also included in the appendix a photocopy of a note from a previous student. This unsolicited heartfelt feedback is one of the greatest rewards an instructor can experience. To have a student ask what other classes you teach so they can have you again, or ask for a letter of recommendation, or to use you as a reference, these are the rewards that mean the most when I look back at my teaching experience. I know that I have earned their respect and admiration while imparting knowledge. (Appendix E)

Appendices

Appendix A: Example of Class Assignment
Appendix B: Student Evaluation Data
Appendix C: Teaching Award
Appendix D: Student Recognition
Appendix E: Example of Unsolicited Student Feedback

TEACHING PORTFOLIO
Ray Shackelford
Department of Industry and Technology
Ball State University

Table of Contents

Teaching Statement and Goal

I am a technology education teacher. By operationalizing this statement I will endeavor to describe what, why and how I teach and my goal as a teacher. *Technology* uses the efficient methods, tools and skills of invention to develop rules and systems for changing knowledge into things done concerning human purposeful activity. Although there is related technology in all disciplines, technology education focuses on technical, human adaptive systems such as communication, construction, manufacturing and transportation. Technology education is *what I teach*.

Webster defines *education* as "the action or process of educating or being educated." The educational system must help all individuals fulfill their needs and reach their fullest potential. This process must

---

Ray Shackelford is Professor of Industry and Technology and has been on the faculty of Ball State University for fifteen years. Previously he taught for five years at New York University.

assist learners to acquire the skill of learning by enhancing their ability to inquire, postulate, reason, make decisions, solve problems, and be independent, self-directed learners. The enjoyment of helping others fulfill their needs and reach their fullest potential is *why I teach*.

Teaching is a series of decisions and a complex social and academic activity. As a *teacher*, I am a key element in the educational system. I have prepared and committed myself to performing the complex task of planning and organizing a comprehensive, flexible, educational environment capable of supporting learner and social needs. Enhancing this environment with instructional strategies capable of supporting educational transmission and transformation is *how I teach*.

Yes, I am a *technology education teacher*. Specifically, a teacher of *future technology education teachers*. Teachers, who will be part of that phase of general education which studies the resources, processes and consequences of technology. Teachers who will help others understand the concepts, principles, interdisciplinary inter-faces and systems of technology, use and control it, analyze and comprehend its consequences, and transfer its knowledge to solve future problems. This is *my goal as a technology education teacher educator*.

Typical Teaching Responsibilities

My primary teaching assignment is in the Department of Industry and Technology. My other duties include assigned time as an Instructional Developer in the Center for Teaching and Learning, Curriculum Coordinator for the teacher education programs in the Department of Industry and Technology, and curriculum specialist for several curriculum development projects. My primary teaching load and area of specialization includes ITEDU 153—*Manufacturing Materials and Processes*, ITEDU 453—*Technical Experiences in Material Processing*, and ITEDU 698—*Seminar in Industrial Education*. My teaching load gives me the opportunity to work with a diversified student population. This is a rewarding experience because it affords me the opportunity to see students develop as they progress through their program.

Teaching Materials

I typically divide teaching materials into two categories: print and non-print. Print materials include course syllabi, exams and handouts. Non-print materials include transparencies, videos and models. All of these materials support the teaching/learning process, but of crucial importance to the process is the course syllabus.

My course syllabi are detailed, written descriptions of the proposed course of study. Putting these details in writing avoids conflict and presents the results of careful planning. I use the syllabus to communicate the course's scope and intent and include information students and colleagues want to know. My syllabi include a course title, catalog description (including credit hours and prerequisites), objectives, rationale and content outline, methods of course and student evaluation, course calendar, and description of the text and other resources. In a course that includes a laboratory experience, laboratory schedules and policies are described. I also include general information about myself, such as office number, hours, and phone number. This makes it easier for students to get in touch with me when questions arise. I often include additional, helpful information such as directions for note-taking, suggested study skills, directions or criteria for learning experiences, a description of the educational environment (e.g., attendance and audit policies), and special considerations for students with special needs (see sample syllabi in Appendix A).

Some print materials such as exams (see Appendix B) and assignments are designed to assess learning, and help me and the students understand their progress toward course objectives (see Appendix C). Other materials such as handouts and non-print materials are used to: (1) show the learner where the lesson is going, (2) simplify complex information, (3) illustrate and emphasize major points, (4) summarize information, or (5) hold the audience's attention (see Appendix D for sample materials).

Efforts to Assess Teaching Effectiveness

Each semester I have all of my courses assessed using selected questions from the "Instructor and Course Appraisal: Cafeteria System." Data from this assessment, illustrated in Figure 1, indicate that students "strongly agree" that (1) teaching methods and materials and (2) course objectives, expectations, content and format are clear, current, well chosen and appropriate to their professional training goals. Median scores on several key questions typically range from 4.6 to 4.9 points on a 5-point scale.

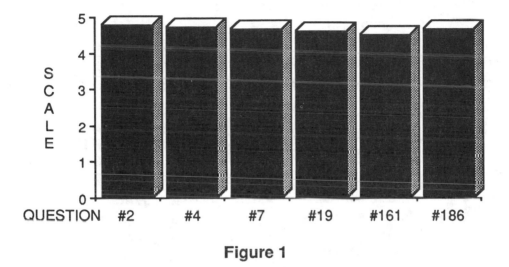

Figure 1

As a teacher, I am pleased to read unsolicited comments made on the back of the student evaluation forms. Selected comments include:

1) "I have found that Dr. Shackelford is very professional and a great professor. I have learned more in his classes than any other."

2) "I would like to thank you for this semester. It has been one of the best and most productive semesters I have ever had. I learned a lot."

3) "You have done something for me: you have got me thinking and gotten me out of a rut."

4) "Dr. Shackelford is the best professor I have ever had. He is well prepared and relates well to students. The work load in this course was vigorous, but effective."

5) "I hold high regard for you. You are one of the best teachers I have ever had. Given the chance, I would like to learn as much as I can from you and hope to model my teaching after yours."

Based upon information gained from the "Cafeteria System" and periodic in-class evaluations, I strive to determine the strengths and weaknesses of my teaching and courses. Then I make required changes to maximize the teaching/learning experience and help students reach both individual and course objectives (see Appendix E for selected course evaluations and student comments).

Efforts to Improve Teaching

As described, teaching is a series of decisions and a complex social and academic activity. It is also a profession and a task that can always be improved upon. Thus, I take advantage of the many opportunities available on campus to improve my teaching, and have attended several presentations on topics sponsored by the Center for Teaching and Learning (see Appendix F). Some of these include:

1) *Learning in Groups* by Dr. Richard Henak, January, 1991.

2) *Effective Discussion Teaching: Lessons from the Case Method* by Dr. William Welty, March, 1990.

3) *Conducting Effective Classroom Discussions* by Dr. Susan Ambrose, November, 1989.

4) *Colleague Evaluation and Student Evaluation* by Dr. Peter Seldin, September, 1989.

5) *Student Involvement: Active Learning in College Classes* by Dr. Peter Fredrick, January, 1989.

I have also attended regional and international conferences specifically designed to enhance teaching. Some of these include conferences sponsored by:

1) *International Technology Education Association (ITEA)*. The ITEA's membership includes secondary and post-secondary technology education teachers from many countries. Conference presentations and discussions focus on current research, strategies, and ideas for implementing technology education programs and enhancing student creativity, decision-making, and problem-solving skills so they can better understand, use, and control technology.

2) *Professional and Organizational Development Network in Higher Education (POD)*. This is a national association devoted to improving teaching and learning in post-secondary education, and provides its members with personal and academic relationships that are essential for professional growth. The conference facilitates the exchange of information and ideas, the development of professional

skills, the exploration and debate of educational issues, and the sharing of expertise and resources.

3) *Lilly Conference on College Teaching*. The Lilly Conference is a national conference giving faculty the opportunity to share proven, innovative pedagogics, and thoughtful, inspirational insights about teaching. Presentations focus on current research, integration of research findings, innovative ideas and strategies, and inspiration for enhancing college teaching.

Future efforts to improve my teaching include plans to invite colleagues to help assess my teaching by observing and videotaping class presentations and reviewing course materials. I have also implemented a Student Quality Control Circle Program. In this program an elected small group of students meets with me to communicate class feedback describing how the class is progressing, whether student needs are being met, and how the teaching/learning process could be enhanced.

Special Teaching and Advising Awards

In 1987, I was recognized by the College of Applied Sciences and Technology for the high-quality educational experience imparted to the students at Ball State University. The award was based upon the results of student and peer evaluations and materials describing the teaching/learning process in my class. As a recipient of this award, I received an increase in my base salary.

In 1989-90, I was honored as the recipient of Ball State's Outstanding Faculty Advisor Award. Honorees receive a substantial one-time cash award. Criteria for the award include: accessibility; knowledge of institutional policies; ability to communicate departmental and institutional goals; ability to establish relationships based on trust and respect; willingness to assist students in assessing their abilities, interests, and limitations; ability to encourage and help students perform to the best of their abilities; and willingness to encourage and help students to become self-directed.

I am particularly pleased with this award because of the strong agreement between its selection criteria and the characteristics of good teaching. These include enthusiasm, clarity, flexibility, organization, fairness, and being warm and approachable (see letters of support in Appendix G).

Another form of special recognition belongs to the departmental program which I coordinate. In 1990, based upon cooperative work of the faculty, the department's Industrial Technology Teacher Education Program became the only fully NCATE accredited technology education program (out of over 35 applicants) in the nation. This honor reflects many years of work and dedication by the department and teacher education faculty (see letters of congratulations in Appendix H).

Teaching-Related Committee Work and Activities

I have recently been elected or appointed to several committees that oversee or impact several faculty development programs and/or undergraduate or graduate teacher education programs on campus. At the departmental level: (1) I was appointed to the Departmental Curriculum Review Committee (approves all course and program changes), (2) I chair the Departmental Teacher Education Curriculum Review Sub-Committee (approves all undergraduate teacher education course and program changes), and (3) I serve as a member of the Departmental Graduate Teacher Education Curriculum Review Sub-Committee (approves all graduate teacher education course and program changes).

At the college level, I was appointed to serve on the university's Teacher Education Committee (approves all undergraduate teacher education course and program changes at the university level).

At the university level I was: (1) elected to the Professional Affairs Council (initiates, monitors, evaluates, and recommends policies regarding faculty appointments, promotion, tenure, benefits, welfare, and grants and awards) and (2) appointed to the Special Leaves Committee (responsible for leaves of absence and sabbaticals).

Other related teaching activities include being selected:
1) as a faculty mentor to three new faculty members;
2) by the Indiana Industrial Technology Education (ITE) Curriculum Committee to coordinate and conduct in-service workshops;
3) to give computer in-service programs for Academic Micro-Computer Software Applications Service Center, BSU;
4) to serve as a member of four doctoral dissertation committees; and
5) as a technology education consultant for the state of Indiana and a number of school, corporation and curriculum projects.

Instructional Developer for the Center for Teaching and Learning, and Teaching the Technology of Teaching (TTT) Program

It is both exciting and rewarding to be part of a university community that has pledged itself to be a premier teaching university. Towards this effort, Ball State has established a variety of excellent faculty development opportunities. As an Instructional Developer for the Center for Teaching and Learning and Director of the Teaching the Technology of Teaching Program, I have had the opportunity to participate in several of these programs (see Appendix I for letters from the Center's Director).

I was instrumental in the development of the TTT Program. Since its inception in 1987, this program has become one of the prominent faculty development programs on campus. Guided by the program's goal to enhance the teaching/learning process, faculty participate in a sequence of twelve seminars designed to help them strengthen their teaching skills and reduce problems often encountered by new faculty who have limited preparation and experience in teaching. However, many faculty have stated that TTT is an excellent program for all faculty. Additionally, participants at the POD and Lilly conferences continue to express a great deal of interest in the program and are impressed by the commitment of our faculty and university to teaching.

Each year faculty apply to participate in the TTT Program. The program is offered Tuesday and Wednesday nights during the Fall Semester and is supported by a series of readings. Based upon positive feedback, this series of readings has been revised and is now distributed to all new faculty under the title *Readings to Help You Enhance Student Learning*.

Indications are that the TTT model for in-servicing new professors is working (see Appendix J for letter from TTT participants). This year several proposals to participate in the program were rejected because of lack of space.

Writings Supporting Good Teaching

To support my teaching and/or the teaching of others, I have been fortunate to recently work on three curriculum development projects. These projects were initiated to develop curriculum guides to support the study of manufacturing systems in the secondary schools. However, the concepts, principles, and activities included in these guides are effective models for introducing related content in many of the technology education classes in the department (see Appendix K).

I have also been involved in a project to develop over 600 technology education activities for secondary schools. These materials are distributed nationwide by the Center for Implementing Technology Education, for which I am Co-Director, with many of the activities used in introductory courses taught in the department and other technology teacher education programs across the country (see Appendix L).

Products of Good Teaching

Most of the courses I teach include a major laboratory component. Thus, many of the student learning experiences culminate in a three dimensional product. Appendix M includes a series of slides illustrating several of the ITEDU 153 learning experiences. These include: (1) manufacturing processes such as permanent and non-permanent mold casting; blanking processes; flexible die and explosion forming; mechanical, adhesion and cohesion assembly; electrical discharge machining; and hot and cold forming processes, (2) material testing activities such as tensile testing; bend testing; and hardness testing, and (3) individual or group activities such as designing and fabricating a bulging flexible die-forming device or a material testing machine capable of doing ten different destructive tests.

Many of the students' testing/processing activities are good enough that they are later published by organizations who distribute technology education activities nationally or are featured in national publications (see Appendix N).

Appendices

Appendix A: Course Syllabi
Appendix B: Sample Tests and Quizzes
Appendix C: Sample Assignments
Appendix D: Non-Print Materials
Appendix E: Student Evaluations
Appendix F: Efforts to Improve Teaching

Appendix G: Teaching/Advising Awards
Appendix H: NCATE Accreditation
Appendix I: Instructional Developer
Appendix J: Teaching the Technology of Teaching
Appendix K: Writings Supporting Good Teaching (Curriculum Guides)
Appendix L: Writings Supporting Good Teaching (Activities)
Appendix M: Products of Good Teaching (Papers and Photographs)
Appendix N: Products of Good Teaching (Published Student Work)

BIBLIOGRAPHY

Berquist, W.H., and Phillips, S.R. A HANDBOOK FOR FACULTY DEVELOP-MENT. Vol. 2, Berkeley, CA: Pacific Soundings Press, 1977.

Bird, T. "The Schoolteacher's Portfolio." In L. Darling-Hammond and J.Millman (Eds.), HANDBOOK ON THE EVALUATION OF ELEMENTARY AND SECONDARY SCHOOLTEACHERS. Newbury Park, CA: Sage, 1989.

Boyer, E.L. SCHOLARSHIP REVISITED. Princeton, NJ: Carnegie Foundation for the Advancement of Teaching, 1990.

Cheney, L.V. TYRANNICAL MACHINES. Washington, DC: National Endowment for the Humanities, 1990.

Edgerton, R. "The Teaching Portfolio as a Display of Best Work." Paper presented at the National Conference of the American Association for Higher Education, Washington, DC, March, 1991.

Edgerton, R. "Report From the President." AAHE BULLETIN, June, 1989, pp. 14-17.

Knapper, C.K. "Evaluation and Teaching: Beyond Lip Service." Paper presented at the International Conference on Improving University Teaching, Aachen, Germany, 1978.

Pascal, C.E. and Wilburn, M.T. "A Mini-Guide to Preparing A Teaching Dossier." ONTARIO UNIVERSITIES PROGRAM FOR INSTRUCTIONAL DEVELOPMENT NEWSLETTER, 1978, 19/20.

Seldin, P. & Associates. HOW ADMINISTRATORS CAN IMPROVE TEACHING. San Francisco: Jossey-Bass, 1990.

Seldin, P. "The Teaching Portfolio." Paper presented at the annual meeting of the Professional and Organizational Development Network in Higher Education, Jekyll Island, GA, 1989.

Seldin, P. "Evaluating Teaching Performance." Workshop presented at the University of Maryland, College Park, MD, 1987.

Seldin, P. SUCCESSFUL FACULTY EVALUATION PROGRAMS. Crugers, NY: Coventry Press, 1980.

Shore, B.M. and others. THE TEACHING DOSSIER, Revised Edition. Montreal: Canadian Association of University Teachers, 1986.

Shulman, L. "Toward a Pedagogy of Substance." AAHE BULLETIN, June, 1989a, pp. 8-13.

Shulman, L. private discussion, 1989b.

Shulman, L. "A Union of Insufficiencies: Strategies for Teacher Assessment in a Period of Educational Reform." EDUCATIONAL LEADERSHIP, November, 1988, 36-41.

Sorcinelli, M.D. EVALUATION OF TEACHING HANDBOOK. Bloomington: Dean of Faculties Office, Indiana University, 1986.

Vavrus, L.G. and Calfee, R.C., Paper presented at the National Reading Conference, Tuscon, AZ, 1988.

INDEX